What Readers of Web Traffic Magnet First Edition said:

"...A Treasure Trove of Traffic Generation Gems..."

- D. Cummings (Cincinnati)

" This book is a MUST!"

- C. Curavo

"Great Book, Amazing info"

- Jesús

"Use it as a checklist against an older site"

- The Happy Artist (Northern New York)

"Lots of good ideas"

- D. Wells (Kansas City, Mo.)

"Terrific Book on SEO"

- A. Johns(NY, NY) -

"Very timely, great tips, easy to read"

- Reader, Puget Sound, WA

"Read once, read again!"

- N. Lohr (New York)

"A Great Little Guidebook"

- M. Nowak (CO, United States)

"Practical, understandable, relevant, useful & easy to read...."

- P. Kane

"Outstanding, concise and easy to implement"

- Jason

"Easy to use guidebook to SEO for any website"

- Zeisel (Seattle WA)

"Concise, complete and practical"

- Kenneth Gillgren

"An SEO book that cuts to the point"

- M. Moshkovich (Los Angeles)

Web Traffic Magnet 2

77 Free Ways to Drive Traffic and
Generate Leads on your Website

Table of Contents

Communications...147

Converting visitors into leads....................................153

Selling from your website..189

*To my father, Seamus Scanlan (1927 – 2011),
who showed me that dreams can come true.*

Introduction

Who is this book for?

Answer: *Anyone who needs to find customers on the Web but who has little or no money to spend doing it.*

I was half way through writing the first draft of this second edition when, one evening I was visiting a local farmers' market, where I bought some hand-made toffee from a local vendor. I looked at the vendor's stall, a little makeshift as you might expect of any stall at a farmers' market, and I wondered how any of these vendors ever made a living. How do they compete with giant confectionery companies? Between the endless sample giveaways, the rent, the transportation and manufacturing costs, how much could there be left to live off? On my just-purchased box of dark chocolate toffee brittle was the URL www.petesperfecttoffee.com and I wondered how on Earth "Pete" could ever afford to generate leads on the Web. His product was the perfect candidate for selling over the Internet – if ever he could afford to connect with potential customers – so it would seem a shame if he missed that huge potential market completely. Then I remembered, there really are many things you can do to a website and on the Web – for absolutely free – to attract and engage potential customers. With that thought, I headed home with the precept to re-focus this book on *what can be done for free* above all else. So you will see that most of the material here – even if it is at times a bit technical – deals with all the *free* things you can do to drive traffic to your website and convert a percentage of those into leads. In addition, if any item is confusing or incomplete, you can contact me at www.sboseries.com where I will try to answer your questions.

Achieving Positive Buoyancy

Have you seen the movie *Das Boot*? There is a scene in it where the submarine is lying on the bottom of the ocean, close to a thousand feet deep – which was *deep* for a submarine in those days – somewhere off Gibraltar. The desperate crew is pumping air into everything they can pump air into, in the hopes that their craft will achieve positive buoyancy. It was an all-or-nothing situation from which, as it turned out, they all survived. It didn't matter that achieving positive buoyancy *just barely worked*. The objective was simply to *achieve positive buoyancy*, even if only by a smidgen. When it comes to making your website appear in *organic search results* (see Glossary page 211), it is like achieving positive buoyancy in the *Ocean of the Internet*. Once you see that first page of your website appearing at the top of search results – for search words that really matter to you – it is highly likely you are witnessing the first signs of success, at least in terms of attracting visitors to your website. What's more, once people begin to click that link to your website in search results, Google (and likely other search engines, because they all emulate Google) adds more weight to your website for the purposes of future appearances in organic search results. *Success begets success:* once you arrive at the surface of organic search results, it is easier to stay there.

Together, we are going to do everything we can to get your website buoyant. That's the first step. Once on the surface, our task turns to capturing the contact information of the visitors we have attracted, while still doing all the things we need to do to stay at the top of search results of course. Capturing contact information is a different type of challenge. The first stage – the *Attract Stage* – is mostly engineering; the second stage – the *Engage Stage* – is mostly marketing. The *Attract Stage* and the *Engage Stage* do overlap a little. You must understand some *marketing* when selecting keywords in the *Attract* Stage, and you must do a little *engineering* to add a contact info gathering form to your website in the *Engage* Stage. I have included references to working samples where it makes sense. And I will answer any additional question you might have on www.sboseries.com.

If only SEO were enough

If a marketing department has any purpose, it is to furnish the sales department with a constant supply of quality sales leads. Just bringing lots of traffic to a website (the SEO or *Search Engine Optimization* part) is not enough anymore – sales people can't do much with website visitors – so this edition of *Web Traffic Magnet* has been expanded to also cover *lead generation*. Lead generation is the primary purpose of a website in almost all small business websites.

In the original edition of this book, published in 2008, I focused on the *Search Engine Optimization* (SEO for short) elements of a successful web presence, but clearly, getting visitors to pass through your website is just the first step. And that first step – SEO – may be the easier step of this two-step challenge. Getting website visitors to offer up their contact information, on the other hand, requires a business owner to wear a different hat, as it were, and most website owners miss the opportunity to convert these visitors into quality leads that can be converted into sales.

To generate leads for what you sell, (a) there must be a market for what you have to offer, (b) you must attract a portion of that market to visit your website, and (c) you must convert a percentage of those to leads. The higher the quality of these leads, the more of them will ultimately become customers.

The following graphics illustrate how a fifty percent improvement over each of the three distinct stages of getting more business on the Web can triple the end result.

Illustration 1 represents how a struggling website loses potential customers are every turn. Their business rarely shows up in search results, so they are unknown to most people in their market. Of those who do find their site, few of them become leads because those visitors get confused, bored or distracted. Of the few leads generated, most are lost due to neglect.

Illustration 2 shows how a modest improvement at each stage can have a profound effect on the overall result, increasing new business on the web by a factor of three.

We are going to try to do a lot more for you than increase each stage's effectiveness by fifty percent. From the years of squeezing out every last drop of web traffic, lead generation and prospect management for my clients and my own businesses, I'm telling you everything I know here.

The illustrations below are fictitious of course but you may be able to do a lot better with the development of your own web presence. Start with the easy stuff in this book; that is, those action items marked with a single ball (one ball denotes easy, five balls denote challenging). Move then to the less easy ones, and so on, and please contact me on www.sboseries.com with any questions you have.

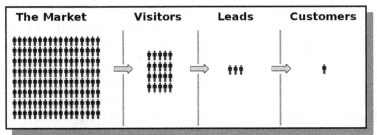

Illustration 1: The three stages of generating new business on the Web. Attract, Engage and Close.

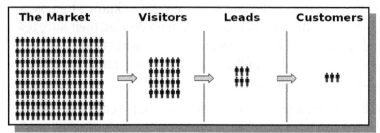

Illustration 2: When each of the three stages (Attract, Engage and Close) is improved by fifty percent, the final sales results are tripled

A common mistake

A common mistake in marketing campaigns on the Web is to skip the lead generation step altogether and try to sell directly to a visitor. Let me give you an example: I was visiting some website or other recently and I saw an ad for the Mercedes C series car across the top 20% of the screen. The graphics were well done and I felt drawn to clicking the image of the pearl-white, sexy automobile. After clicking the ad, the browser took me to another website. Instead of inviting me to request a brochure or to view more images or something, the page tried to sell me a car. It went straight from introduction to talking about pricing and placing an order. I lost interest and clicked the Back button on my browser and continued whatever I was doing before I saw the ad. What happened? Instead of developing a relationship with me by offering me one of those sweet-smelling car brochures in the mail, or inviting me to sign up for pre-announcements of future cars or something, they tried to close the deal. They thought they could dispense with the notion of relationship development and ask me to *come home with them before we ever went on a date*.

Even if you are Mercedes-Benz, securing a new customer requires that you develop a relationship first; that is, the *Engage Stage*. It might be *easier* for Mercedes-Benz – due to their strong brand – to engage a prospect, but even they can't skip the step altogether.

What has changed?

The physics of attracting visitors to a website has not changed in over a decade; it is just that there are more things you can do today than there were then. For example, Twitter was only coming of age in 2008, and Facebook hadn't touched mainstream business like it does today. In addition, travelers on the Web are more savvy now, more discriminating and more wary of identity theft, phishing and scams of one type or another, so *trust* will play a more significant role in any success you hope to have. The big search engines – Google, Bing, Yahoo, etc. – are also more aware of the tireless armies of interlopers on the Web who try to 'game the system' to drive search traffic to their own websites, but without adding real value to visitors' experience. As the online market for almost everything grows bigger each year, both sides of this equation can also be expected to grow. With all that noise around us, the principles of delivering customer value have not changed, and that's what this book is about: delivering value to customers.

An organization's website is a kind of resumé; a vehicle to begin a deep and long-lasting relationship with those who need what the organization has to offer. Any good recruiter will tell you that a resumé must, above all, be honest. It is the same with how you use your website – and indeed, your entire web presence – as a foundation for how you connect with and grow productive relationships with the outside world.

And so, this book is about putting your organization's best foot forward. If there is a market for what you deliver, together we will allow the world to find you. They will see who you are and they will embrace the value of your product or service. To that end, all of the action items in this book are about showing to the world the best of what you have to offer, rather than gaming the system to generate more traffic or sales leads.

The practice of generating website traffic by adding value to visitors' experience is called *White Hat.* Its alter ego *Black Hat*, on the other hand, is the name given to the myriad ways of tricking search engines to do ones bidding. Only *White Hat* served here.

I want to offer you *more for less*. With this second edition of Web Traffic Magnet, I list more actions you can take, go into more detail with each, and explain most technical terms in a *Glossary of Terms*, beginning on page 205, and I provide a website to support this and other books in the *Small Business Owner Series* at www.sboseries.com. You are invited to visit me there and ask any question, share your experiences, or contribute to other discussions if you wish.

Some of the actions are more technical than others. I try to explain them in terms that will make sense to the average business person who does not have an engineering degree.

Still, you may prefer to hand part of this over to your website administrator or your hosting company. Hopefully, though, you will understand each action item *enough* to see where it fits into the big picture of your success on the Internet.

The good news

The basic principles of Search Engine Optimization (SEO) have not changed much since the late 1990s. And, contrary to how many would have you believe, the art and science of making more visitor traffic flow through your website is quite easy to understand. At least, each piece of it is easy to understand. There are, however, dozens and dozens of actions to take. The good news is, you can do most of them yourself, without the help of a deeply skilled technician or an expensive consultant. It turns out, the most effective methods of attracting traffic are often the easiest ones to implement. The bad news is, if there indeed is any, more organizations – your competitors come to mind – are today all doing the easy things, so the fight has shifted to the harder-to-do action items.

Let's look at an example:

When my friend Cory and I started Bocada in July 1999, we simultaneously worked on both our product and our website for about eighteen months, which was how long it took to release our first product. Our website had about eight pages of content and a way for visitors to enter their contact information which was then inserted into a table in a database by an invisible script behind the website. For those eight pages, I made sure the page names, titles, descriptions and body text all contained keywords relating to our subject matter: our up-and-coming product. Of course, the content itself needed also to be of value to visitors – a list of about ninety features of backup products, together with a check mark beside each mainstream product that supported that feature – so enough of them were interested enough to provide to us their basic contact information. By listing all of the main features of data backup products, the website naturally captured most of the keywords people were likely to use when they searched for a solution related to what we were doing. The year was 1999 and it was the first time I had ever created a true Search Engine Optimized website, complete with Target Landing Pages and a way to capture visitor contact information.

Today, the same basic principles are used to achieve the same type of result. As a test of how little things have changed – by the latter half of 2011 – I created a website from scratch for a friend of mine who hand-builds professional racing bicycles. We came up with a company name (Kirkland Cycle), a domain name (kirklandcycle.com) and a dozen keywords relating to his business. I built a simple, ten-page website, including a blog to which he added ten blog postings. Within three weeks, his phone started to ring, and he began closing business with real, paying customers.

In the first eighteen months of Bocada's existence – spanning July 1999 to about February 2001 – our simple website collected the contact information of more than *seven hundred visitors*. Most of them were the Who's Who in the world of global corporations and domestic behemoths. That database of leads was to serve the company for the next half-dozen years, bringing Bocada's annual revenue close to ten million dollars before we employed additional means of generating quality sales leads.

Today, in the second decade of the twenty-first century, there are many more bits and pieces that go into SEO – just like motor cars are significantly more complex under the hood today than they were fifty years ago – but like today's average gasoline-fueled automobile, the principles have not changed.

Generating revenue through your web presence involves three stages: *Attract, Engage* and *Close*. You *Attract* visitors to your website, *Engage* them sufficiently to convert some visitors into leads, then *Close* the sales deal by making them a customer at some point beyond that. This book covers the *Attract* and *Engage* stages: getting the right type of visitor to look at your website and capturing their contact and profile information for later use in sales.

How to use this book

Each action item can be taken as a discrete suggestion. In other words, you don't have to read this book in any particular order; you can start right away with action item 42, then jump back to number 11, and so on.

Like most things in life, not everything you do to generate website traffic gives you the same return on invested effort. To help you decide which items you wish to work on first, I have included an *Effort / Cost / Reward* table for each action item. You may wish to scan through the high reward items first, regardless of Effort level, if you have some basic technical skills. Or, if you want to practice making improvements first, begin by selecting items with a low Effort rating.

I have also grouped at the beginning all of the actions that don't require you to spend money. I know that cash flow is often of critical importance in small companies, so let's see if we can make a difference to your website traffic before you spend any more money.

Each action item is preceded by an *Effort / Cost / Reward* table like this one:

Effort is indicated as a level of difficulty between 1 and 5, where 1 is easy and 5 is more challenging.

You don't have to be a computer programmer to make any of these changes. Even the most difficult action fits within the classification of "between beginner and intermediate", as indicated on the front cover. Some of the recommended actions, you should be able to pass to your website hosting company or website administrator. If you get stuck or simply have a question, you can contact me at: www.sboseries.com.

Listed beside each action is a number of stars to denote the relative value of taking that action. For example, making sure every page's *title tag* is done right gets five stars because it can – on its own – improve a page's search results position significantly.

Some actions may have only a marginal effect on website traffic generation, while others might have a profound effect. Interestingly, the more difficult actions are not necessarily those that have the greatest effect. For example

– as alluded to in the previous paragraph – every page in a website can have its own title, identified by what is called the *title tag*. This title tag has probably the single largest influence on how a given page is matched up with search words – and thus, it a major influence on where in search results its page will appear – but it is one of the easiest things on a website to change. That is why it gets a five-star Reward label and an Effort level of 1.

Here is an example of an action that is very easy to implement, but may have a very positive effect on the respective page's position in search results:

22. Include keywords in page title

Effort: ●○○○○	Cost: $0	Reward: ★★★★★

If the tool you use to maintain your website allows you to enter a title for each page, add at least a few keywords to the beginning of the title on each page. If you use an HTML Editor like Notepad or such, the line in question will look like this. Notice how the keywords are placed at the start of the title:

```
<title>bicycle, bike, manhattan, service, repair ::
Welcome to Manhattan Bicycle Inc.</title>
```

Whatever program you use to maintain your web pages, the end result should look like the highlighted text, above, when you view the source for that page in a browser. To see an example in the real world, browse to www.ibm.com and use the browser menu to view the source code. (*View/Source* in Internet Explorer, or *View/Source Code* in Firefox).

Introduction

The single ball to the right of the word *Effort*: tells us that the action is easy to do. The five stars at the end of the description tells us the payoff may be high.

The combination of difficulty level and potential return on effort will help you decide which actions to focus on first.

- The first section, *Increasing website traffic without spending money,* deals with actions that can be done without spending any money, usually through your Web Content Management System or using your browser to change content on other people's websites.

- The next section, *Spending a little money,* covers those actions that may cost a *little* money. For example, buying a few more years of domain name may cost you thirty dollars.

- The next section, *Spending more money: Google AdWords,* is for those with an advertising budget.

- *Communications* deals with managing communication with visitors, "Followers", "Likers", leads and customers on the Web, including on your own website and in what are sometimes called "Social Media" communities like Facebook and Twitter.

- *Converting visitors into leads* covers what to do with the website visitor traffic you generate. A visitor, after all, isn't worth much unless you can get their contact information and begin a relationship that will ultimately result in doing business with a portion of them. That second step or "stage", *converting visitors into leads,* is often neglected as people understandably rush to try closing business with visitors, or worse, ignore their website visitors entirely.

Of the three distinct stages of closing business on the Web, this book focuses primarily on the first stage, the *Attract* stage, and secondarily on the *Engage* stage. The third stage, that of actually closing the sale, is up to you, the business owner.

Introduction

Increasing website traffic without spending money

1: First things first. Getting a health check

Effort: ●○○○○	Cost: $0	Reward: ★★★

Before you make any changes to your website, it would be nice to have a way to measure its current condition. As it happens, there is such a way. The good folks at HubSpot offer a free, online website grading tool that gives you a kind of "search engine score". The great thing about it is, it's a *percentile* score, which means it measures your website on a scale containing the scores of millions of other websites. If you get a score of 75%, it means that your website is "better than 75% of the millions of websites they know about".

To measure your website's current score:

1. Visit www.WebsiteGrader.com

2. Enter your website address

3. Press the orange button

Make a note of the score you receive. We will return here occasionally to see how it improves as we progress through all the changes we make.

Note that WebsiteGrader may not retest your website if you try the test too soon after the last time you did it. In such cases, it may give to you the same score it calculated earlier in the day. So think about checking it again the following day.

2: Executing a Long Keyword Strategy

Effort: ●●○○○   Cost: $0   Reward: ★★★★

"And the third bowl of porridge was just right"
- Goldilocks, after tasting Baby Bear's porridge

A "hot" keyword is a term that is searched for so often that only large, established websites are likely to appear at the top of search results when people use it to search the Web. For example, if you Google the word *jewelry*, which is such a hot keyword, you are likely to see only famous brand name stores and businesses at the top of organic search results. That is because – among other reasons – the keyword *jewelry* is very commonly searched for, so the competition for any website to appear at the top of search results is significant. Other examples of hot keywords are *ipad, airline, vacation, harry potter,* and so on. As you might have guessed, a "cold" keyword (or "long" keyword) is one that is searched for *infrequently*. For example, the following four words entered together into Google search represent a *cold keyword*: *reflexology services bellevue washington*. That is because that exact combination of words is searched for perhaps only a few hundred times over the course of a year.

Using predominantly *cold keywords* - for which there is significantly less competition and are therefore easier to attract website traffic with – is to adopt a *long keyword strategy*, a term you will see more and more often in this era of Internet business. More on that a few paragraphs down...

There are two easy ways to expand your list of possible keywords to use in the construction of each of your *Target Landing Pages*. (More on *Target Landing Pages* on page 158). One is to use *Google Sets*, outlined on page 52. The other is to use the *Google AdWords* application to see how many searches – across all searches performed through the Google search engine – are being performed on the keywords you currently plan to use, and also to see some alternative keyword suggestions. We do this using the *Google Keyword Tool*, and this is how:

To use the *Google Keyword Tool*, which is free by the way, visit www.google.com/adwords and click the menu bar *Reporting and Tools / Keyword Tool* as shown in Illustration 3 on page 30.

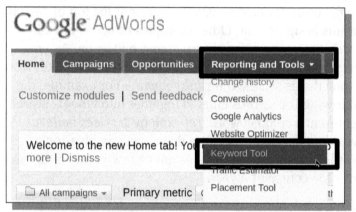

Illustration 3: Visit www.google.com/adwords and select the Keyword Tool as shown. You may have to create an account to proceed to this step.

Note: Screen designs change so frequently on the Web that the location of the *Google Keyword Tool* may be different by the time you read this. Still it's usually only a case of sniffing around a bit to find where it is currently located. It also might be renamed, so keep your eye open for that too.

Illustration 4 on page 35 shows the number of searches performed in Google using the words *plumber seattle*. In the typical local search type of words (e.g. *pizza lower manhattan* or *plumber seattle*) the number of searches performed *globally* will be almost the same as the number of searches performed *locally*. That is because local searches are usually not performed outside a small geographical region. For example, *pizza lower manhattan* is unlikely to be Google'd in Houston, Texas.

Do your customers generally live within driving distance of your business? In other words, would they *drive to your business* to buy your product or service? If the answer is Yes, then you will be interested in the number represented by **(d)** in Illustration 4 on page 35. That is, you are interested in how many *Local Monthly Searches* are performed on the keywords you are interested in. If your customers are generally *not within driving distance* – that is, your market is national or global – the number that is important to you is that represented by **(c)** in Illustration 4 on page 35. That number is important because it is the "total number of fish in the lake" that you can capture with the "fish lure you are using". In other words, you will be aiming to capture a subset of that number of searches with a Target Landing Page on your website specifically designed to capture *those exact searches*.

The important point here is to examine how many searches are performed using the keywords *you* think are likely to be used to find a page on *your* website in *your* target market. If the words you entered into the Google Keyword Tool, as shown in Illustration 4 on page 35 (represented by **(c)** or **(d)**, depending on whether your market is non-local or local, respectively) give you a high number, then your challenge to appear early in search results is greater. What constitutes a "high number" depends on many things, including how big and how profitable your market is, but my rule-of-thumb is – if you are a small business – aim for keywords that give you less than 10,000 searches in your target market. You can create five different Target Landing Pages – in your blog, for instance – each using keywords that give you a low number in Google Keywords Tool (like those shown in Illustration 4 on page 35) and have a higher chance of capturing website traffic with each, rather than making your keywords shorter, in an attempt to capture more traffic on a single Target Landing Page. In other words, we want to have an easy job of capturing a less frequently searched for term, rather than a tough time competing for website traffic from high volume search words.

When my twelve year-old son and I go fishing in Lake Washington, we have no idea what kind of fish there are in the lake, so we don't target any particular breed. We have caught two fish in perhaps five years. Last summer, there was another person fishing alongside us at our favorite spot. He had three different lines in the water, and within the hour he was there beside us, he had caught perhaps a dozen fish, a few on each of the lines he had in the water. We got to talking with him and he explained that each line had a different type of lure – one for each of three different types of fish he was there to catch that day. It was a great lesson for my son and me: the lesson was, *each specific type of fish required a different lure*. We, on the other hand, were trying to catch "any fish" and ended up capturing none.

It is the same with how you design your keywords for a *Target Landing Page*. The closer you match its keywords with a specific search performed on the Web, the more likely you are to catch something.

To summarize the points of the previous paragraphs:

1. A Target Landing Page is designed to capture a specific search term, just like a key is designed to open a specific lock.

2. The lower the number of searches performed using a given keyword, the more likely a page designed specifically to that keyword will appear at the top of search results and thus, drive traffic to your website.

3. Your keyword strategy is *page*-based, not *website*-based. That means, you match a page up with a desired keyword, and not try to "get the whole website to match up with your list of keywords". The overall search engine stickiness (see more on what that means on page 213) of your website will help each individual page of course – a rising tide raises all boats, as they say – but consider each Target Landing Page to be a discrete project for the purposes of generating web traffic. (Details on how to design Target Landing Pages on page 158).

Increasing website traffic without spending money

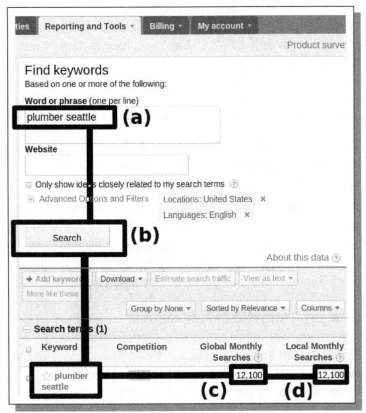

Illustration 4: the Google Keyword Tool allows you to see how many actual searches are performed using the keywords you are considering.

For example: In the company *Kirkland Cycle*, instead of a single Target Landing Page on your website attempting to capture all bicycle-related searches in Kirkland City, you might create one for the keyword *kirkland bicycle repairs*, another for *kirkland bicycle rentals* and another for *kirkland bicycle training courses.* Each of those three keywords (or key *phrases*, really) is "colder" than the potential keywords *kirkland bicycle.* There is simply less competition for such "colder" keywords – because there are fewer searches for them and fewer pages match them well – so a page that *does* match it well is *significantly* more likely to appear on Page One of search results.

In addition to seeing how "hot" or "cold" your keywords might be, the Google Keyword Tool also gives you alternatives to the words you have chosen.

Several of my clients compete with some very large corporations. In every case, we were able to get my client ahead of their behemoth competitors by using this *long keyword strategy.* In reality, though, each of my clients is competing with a *small part* of their huge competitor, and the *long keyword strategy* reflects the fact that we were competing with a sliver of the competitor's business. The long keyword strategy is the way a small company competes with a huge, dominant, established player in the market and it is one of the most exciting opportunities presented to us by the arrival of the Internet.

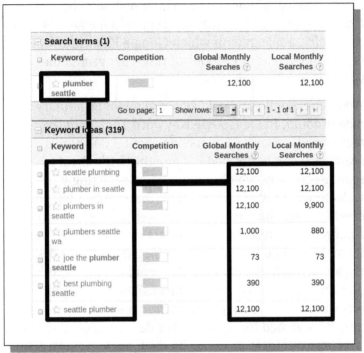

Illustration 5: Scrolling down on the Google Keyword Tool will show you alternative keyword combinations to consider.

The keyword *seattle plumber,* when entered into the Google Keyword Tool returns about 12,000 searches, as you can see in Illustration 5. That means, people on the Internet use Google to search using those exact words about 12,000 times per month. At 12,000, I would classify this as a "warm" keyword for which there will be some competition among plumbers in the Seattle area, but which would still remain a possibility for a company who wanted to use it to try driving traffic to their own website. Compare that number with the result of a *hot keyword* such as *jewelry*, a search term which Google Keyword Tool says is performed tens of millions of times per year in the Google search engine alone.

Another example of a *cold keyword* might be *military memorabilia*. In the Google Keyword Tool, *military memorabilia* shows up as having about 3,600 global searches being performed per month. That's about ten searches per day, which is not a lot, considering your website will only get a fraction of that number, but you can create a single blog page on your website designed to capture search results for that exact term. But wait, there's more. You could have a hundred blog pages, each designed to capture each of a hundred such cold keywords. Where do you find the hundred cold keywords? In the Google Keyword Tool. The keyword *military memorabilia* might only be searched for ten times per day, but look at the other *cold keyword* ideas provided by the Google Keyword Tool, shown in Illustration 6 on page 39. By the way, the horizontal bar in the Competition column refers to how expensive Google AdWords are likely to be if you bid for placement using that keyword. We, on the other hand, are trying to get our web page to appear in the *organic* section of search results, below or to the left of the ads.

Keyword ideas (327)		
Keyword	Competition	Global Monthly Searches
military emblems		12,100
military products		12,100
army items		12,100
military accessories		9,900
marine gifts		9,900
militaria wwii		9,900
4 armed forces		8,100
military stuff		8,100
military tees		8,100
military collectibles		8,100
military figurines		8,100
german ww2 uniforms		6,600
ww2 uniforms german		6,600

*Illustration 6: The Google Keyword Tool may offer hundreds of other ideas, and alternatives to the search terms **military memorabilia**.*

Why does Google almost always display my Home Page in search results, rather than my Target Landing Page?

Sometimes, Google will display in search results the Home Page of a website instead of what might seem to be a far more highly targeted page on the same website. I never worked out for sure why this happens, so I will give you my educated guess: The Home Page on a website often has a much higher Google PageRank than many of the individual pages on the same site. It may be that, even though a specific page on your website seems to you to be a far better match to a given set of search words, Google – or any other search engine – may prefer to display your Home Page because of that higher PageRank or because the Home Page is more likely to be around for a lot longer than an individual page. Another reason might be – and this again is a bit of a guess – more than one of the pages on your website might be a good match for the search in question, so rather than decide which one to display in search results, Google displays your Home Page.

3: The easiest way to blog every day

Effort: ●●○○○   Cost: $0   Reward: ★★★★

Guess a couple of your favorite keywords and enter them into search. Scan the resulting list of web pages and pick one that looks like it might be a decent article on the subject. Read the first few sentences and paraphrase them in a new entry to your blog. Add a link back to the original article, save your work to the website, and the blog posting is finished.

How long did that take? About five minutes. The material you have used is not original, but you have given full credit back to the originating website where you found it. By doing that, you have – in the view of search engines – added some value to the website that owns the original content and satisfied your own website's need for new daily content.

For example: Imagine you have an online golf products store and are struggling to come up with new material to blog about every day. Google "golf enthusiast" and scan the search results until you find an article of interest. Take note of its URL (e.g. http://mygolfpages.blogspot.com/swing.html). On your own blog, create a new posting of about two sentences, summarizing the article you have found. Link from your new blog posting back to the article you found.

There is more detail on the subject of long keyword strategy starting from page 28, including screen captures of the Google Keyword Tool and how to use it see how effective your keywords are likely to be.

4: Doing blog postings in batches

Most Web Content Management Systems today offer the ability to schedule the publication of a blog posting (or any new page) to your website at a specified time and date in the future.

> Create twelve or more blog postings in one sitting and schedule them to publish one a day for twelve days in a row. Do more at the same time if you have the energy.

It is easier to do a dozen blog postings in a single sitting than do one a day for twelve days.

5: Blogging about what you know

Effort: ●●○○○	Cost: $0	Reward: ★★★★☆

Every business owner I know has in his or her head a treasure trove of wisdom about their business and the market they are in. Each nugget of wisdom can form the basis of an individual blog posting.

Giving the game away

When I write a book, I try to include in it everything I know on the subject. People have often said they were puzzled by my divulging all my "secrets". Well, they're not *my* secrets; they are information I discovered on my own journey with my readers, my clients and my business. Many people around the world know what I know – at least, collectively they do – so I am only divulging what is already known somewhere in the world. The way I look at it is, if ways of driving traffic to your website are to be explained in a book, I'd like to be the person to do it.

Think about your own business for a moment. What do you know about your industry that would be of interest to visitors – potential customers – to your website? A plumber friend of mine said to me the other day that he *never does plumbing work in a bathroom until tile grouting work has settled for at least three days*. This nugget of wisdom is an example of an ideal blog posting on a plumber's website. Another one he told me was that he *always uses a wide bend in sewer pipes instead of sharp bends. It reduces the chances of a blockage, and makes it easier to fix if one occurs*. That snippet, too, could make another excellent blog posting.

Can you identify a dozen pieces of wisdom about your particular business? Begin with twelve, and don't worry about spilling secrets. Someone else will, if you don't.

6: Blogging about what you don't know

Effort: ●●●○○ | Cost: $0 | Reward: ★★

This is more challenging than writing about a subject you are very familiar with. Still, a little research can get you great material for writing blogs on a subject you are not familiar with, and may help those readers who are creating blog content for a client whose business is unfamiliar.

Visit your local library and take a dozen books on the subject to a table. Scan them for snippets of knowledge and use each snippet as its own blog posting on your website. When you take substantial information from a book, give credit to the book author in your blog posting.

The hard part is just getting some basic piece of material written. Often, the owner of the business – or a subject matter expert on staff – may find it far easier to make a few adjustments or edits to your work, once that initial creation is done.

7: Using dashes rather than underscores in URL names

Effort: ●●○○○ | Cost: $0 | Reward: ★★

> Where you get the opportunity to choose dashes between words in URLs, use them instead of underscores.

It can't be proven either way, but many people believe Google prefers dashes in URLs over the use of underscores.

In other words, the keywords *bicycle, manhattan* and *rentals* are easier for Google to identify in the URL (or file name) *bicycle-rentals-manhattan.html* than they are in *bicycle_rentals_manhattan.html*.

Many Web Content Management Systems (WCMs) allow you to specify which separator character to use during the automatic creation of new pages on the website. If your WCM does offer the feature, set the character to *dash* (-) instead of *underscore* (_).

8: Blog posting with backlink from someone else's blog

 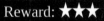

Effort: ●●●○○   Cost: $0   Reward: ★★★☆☆

The most important aspect of posting to someone else's blog is that you include a link from it back to your own website.

> First, do a search of the Internet to find a forum that accepts entries from outsiders. If you are in the online counseling profession, you might search using the words *counseling relationships forum*. Scan the list of search results that are displayed for a website that allows you to register and contribute an article or answer someone

else's question. If you have not already done so, register and look in the forum for either:

a question you can answer using your expertise or

a topic on which you can write a short article.

In either case, be sure to add a link back to your website from the blog posting.

This increases the number of links back to your website which may result in driving visitors to your website simply because they follow your link. Sometimes, such a link also contributes credibility – in the view of search engines – to your website in terms of backlink count and keyword reinforcement. More on that in the point relating to something called the *nofollow* tag on page 48.

9: Placing keywords in page titles

This action item involves the least amount of work (one ball) and has the highest reward (five stars).

Every page on your website can have a page title. The page title is probably the single most important object – in the view of search engines – for matching search words with actual pages on the Web. Surprisingly, and to your advantage, many websites still ignore this great opportunity. The page title is as important to a web page as the title of a resumé is to candidate seeking a job. Just as a resumé titled *Welcome to my resumé* will hinder a candidate's chances of getting that first interview, a page titled *Welcome to Acme Products* tells search engines nothing about the possible contents of a web page.

At the risk of mixing my metaphors, imagine for a moment each page on your website is a kind of search engine lottery ticket. Each one is another chance to attract search traffic. You should have a variety of them, each with its own chance of winning a piece of traffic coming from search engines. Consider the following page titles for three web pages on the same website:

1. Bicycle sales, service and repair in Kirkland, Redmond, Seattle.

2. Kirkland bike sales, rental and repair.

3. Seattle bike/bicycle repair and rental.

Even though three different people are looking for the same thing, they might search for it in different ways. Depending on the exact order and content of a specific search, Google may match it with any one of the three example above. For example, a person who Googles *kirkland bike repair* might see page number 2, above, whereas someone who Googles *bicycle repair kirkland* might see page number 1, at the top of search results. By offering search engines variations in page titles in your website, you increase the chances that at least one of your web pages will appear at the top of search results. Remember too that search engines give more weight to the words at the beginning of the page title than those in the middle or at the end. Keywords separated by commas tell search engines which words are part of the same keyword. For example: *kirkland, bicycle rentals.*

1. Every page on your website should contain keywords relating to the page it is on.

2. Have a variety of keyword combinations across page titles on your web pages.

3. Place your keywords within the first ninety characters of the page title. Search engines often ignore anything beyond that.

4. Place your most important keywords at the beginning.

5. Separate keywords with commas.

Page *titles* and page *headers* often get confused by people managing their websites, so let's look at how you know what the exact title of a page is: As you look at a web page on the Internet, its page title is the text *in the colored bar at the top of the browser*. Illustration 7 shows a browser window with two tabs open. The title of the current page is displayed in the colored bar at the top of the window, and the title of each open page is displayed in its respective tab. Note, by the way, that the Common Dreams website does not appear to have keywords in their page title. That might be OK, because they have an established brand and may consider *common dreams* to be more likely what people will search for.

Increasing website traffic without spending money

Illustration 7: The title of the current page is displayed in the top bar of the browser and in the tab bar of the page.

10: Posting only to non *nofollow* tag websites

Effort: ●●●○○	Cost: $0	Reward: ★★★☆☆

Backlinks vary in value. A backlink on the home page of IBM's website back to your website would be extremely valuable to you, especially if you were in the kind of business that caters to the typical visitor of IBM's website. That is because a page on IBM's website is likely to have a lot of *search engine stickiness*. On the other hand, a backlink from a static, unknown website with little traffic would not be of value to your website.

Here are the factors that affect the value of a backlink:

1. How heavily trafficked is the website it is coming from?

2. Is the website content closely related to your business? A link from the Crochet Society of

America will add little value to your Harley-Davidson dealership website.

3. How valuable do search engines believe the website is? (e.g. what is its Google PageRank, how many backlinks does it have pointing to it, and so on). Websites of higher perceived value "feed" the value of your website.

4. Does the website use the *nofollow* tag to limit the value it send to the website it is linking to?

The *nofollow* tag, when placed near the link to your website, tells search engines "this is not an endorsement of the website we are linking to". In other words, search engines do not give your website credit for the backlink even though it links directly to your website.

Before you make a posting to a particular website/forum with a view to including a backlink, determine if the website uses the *nofollow* tag. This is how:

Most browsers allow you to view the HTML source of any page you visit on the Web. Firefox (a popular Web browser) allows you to view the source for whatever piece of a web page you have just selected. Browse to a page on the forum that contains a backlink that a previous contributor has added. Take a note of the link and use the browser's View menu to view the source for the page. Even if you have never looked at HTML before, with all that gobbledygook in front of you, search for the word "nofollow", just like it is spelled in Illustration 8. If you see the word anywhere within the source code, likely the website is using it to tell search engines not to pass value to any website that it links to.

At this point, you can decide whether you want to still go ahead and add a blog posting, create a forum topic or answer a question on this website, but at least you know what you are getting for your work. Sometimes it is still worth it, because you get your name in front of visitors to that website, or you drive some visitors to your website because they click your link.

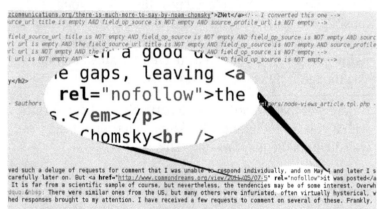

Illustration 8: An example of source code for a page, showing a link that uses the nofollow tag.

11: Using *anchor text* in your backlink

Effort: ●○○○○	Cost: $0	Reward: ★★★☆☆

We know that search engines use the content on a website to reinforce keyword likelihood on a website it links to. For example, if you ran a golf product store on the Web, a link from the official PGA Tournament's website to yours could add enormous value to your website when it comes to keywords. It does it in two ways:

(1) A preponderance of golf-related words on the PGA website increases the likelihood that *your* website will come up for golf-related search words because of the link from the PGA's website to yours. It is *keyword relevance by association*.

(2) Anchor text gives a strong indication of what subject matter the destination website contains.

Anchor text is best described using an example. The first of these does not use anchor text; the second does.

1. This is about computers: www.ibm.com

2. This is about computers.

The second link gives the search engines that are examining the web page a clue about what might be on the web page it links to. The first link just shows the URL of the destination page.

When you are adding a link from someone else's page to yours, use anchor text if possible. This means, before you press the save button on your blog posting on the external website, you select the plain language text itself and click a link button that allows you to enter the URL of your own website.

12: Linking from pages with few links

Effort: ●○○○○	Cost: $0	Reward: ★★★☆☆

Links from a valuable website add value to any website they point to, but what if there are links on a single page to thousands of other websites? Does the same value flow out to each destination page as would flow if there were just one link? The short answer is No.

Imagine a particular web page's *search engine stickiness* were ten dollars. Search engines divide that value across all of the pages it links to, so if a page already has dozens of outbound links on it, understand that a link you add from it to your website will receive only a sliver of the original *search engine stickiness*. It still might be worth it, though. I would be very happy if a link to my website were one of a thousand from a web page with a Google PageRank of 9.

13: Google Sets: expanding your list of keywords

Effort: ●○○○○	Cost: $0	Reward: ★★★☆☆

If you owned a furniture store, it might be hard to get beyond the obvious *couch, chair, table, sofa* and *love seat*, so how else can you find keywords that people might use to find your business? It is usually a struggle to come up with a good, long list of keywords relating to content on your website. What's more, scanning a thesaurus, as well as being labor-intensive, only gives you words that the *thesaurus* believes are synonyms. Wouldn't it be more interesting to know what *Google* believes are the synonyms for the keywords you already have?

There are tools and services available to comb through your website and provide you with a list if keyword candidates, taken directly from your web pages, but what about potential keywords you have never used?

Take those first five words you know about in your business. In the furniture store example, it might be *couch, chair, table, sofa* and *love seat*. Visit the URL ***http://labs.google.com/sets*** and enter them into the five boxes – it should look something like Illustration 9, below – then press the *Large Set* button. If you can't think of your best five words, use the furniture example. When you see the result in a moment, you may be inspired to think of five words relating to your own business.

Illustration 9: Enter your five "best guess" keywords into Google Sets and press Large Set

The long list of related words it provides is not just pulled from some static thesaurus or database. It is a list of *semantically related keywords* that Google has determined are often found in the same context. I can't say for certain, but I would not be surprised to learn that Google used this data to improve search results by including websites that contain such semantically related keywords. That is because no one can really determine what exact words a given person is going to use to search the Internet. The only way to determine it is to examine vast amounts of data and detect patterns of word use. That's a job for some very brainy people and Google certainly appears to have done it.

Let's consider a theoretical example. An online discussion forum, majoranalysis.com gets posted to daily – sometimes every few minutes – by contributors across the English-speaking world and beyond. Where contributors from the United States might use the word *situationalize,* an Australian might use the word *imagine*. A Canadian might use the word *sofa,* whereas a Californian might use the word *couch*. The huge volume of content on, for example, the majoranalysis.com website provides the typical kind of data that search engines use to work out such *semantically related keywords.*

In this action item, we are simply piggy-backing Google's hard work by using the Labs feature to provide us with words we are unlikely to come up with ourselves, but are the actual words Google is likely to match against, when people do a search on the Web.

14: Unifying your domain name

More often than not, a website's domain name is split in two as far as search engines are concerned.

To look at a fictitious example, www.myfancywebsite.com and myfancywebsite.com (without the 'www.') are seen as two different websites. Any *search engine stickiness* the owner of the website creates for it will be divided between the two addresses. It is better when search engines consider them both to be the same website, combining the strength of the backlinks and other good stuff into a single website focal point. To combine both into one, we do a *Permanent 301 Redirect* on one to the other.

To add a Permanent 301 Redirect to merge the value of the "two websites" into one, we go to the cPanel (the Control Panel on your website hosting account) and add it there. It is quite easy to do if you are at all familiar with the cPanel but it might be just as easy to ask your Webmaster or the company that hosts your website to do it for you. The screen that allows you to add a *Permanent 301 Redirect* will be similar to that shown in Illustration 10 on page 57.

Your hosting company and/or your Webmaster will point you to where cPanel (hosting Control Panel) is located. Although the step is easy to take, it is advisable to make this change only if you are familiar with how cPanel works.

Some organizations prefer to point the URL with the 'www.' to point to the URL without the 'www.'. For example, the community website Twitter.com does that. To see it happening, type www.twitter.com into your browser address bar and you will see it redirect to the address *without* the www. Mostly, though, organizations like to keep the 'www.' in their website's address. Whichever one you choose, add the *Permanent 301 Redirect* to unite both websites.

Illustration 10: Using cPanel to add a Permanent 301 Redirect to point the domain name to the website. This makes search engines see both as the same website.

15: Adding Google Analytics to your website

Effort: ●●●○○ Cost: $0 Reward: ★★★

Google Analytics sounds a bit high tech, but it's easy to use and can provide valuable and interesting insights into what is happening on your website. For the average webmaster, it takes a few minutes to install, and you only have to do it once, so you might consider giving the task to your web person if you prefer. There are no special instructions; you simply have to request that Google Analytics is installed in every page of the website. You will learn:

- Which search words people are using to find your website

- Which pages are getting the most traffic

- What percentage of visitors are from search engines, advertisements, links from elsewhere and direct visits (where they type in your website's address)

- Is traffic increasing or decreasing over time?

- How many visitors go away after looking at one page? (It is called the "bounce rate").

- How long do visitors stay on the site?

- Exactly how many visitors did I get from a specific ad I placed online?

- Which blog postings (or product pages) generate the most traffic from search engines?

How to install Google Analytics:

Search Google for the words "google analytics" and follow the link, or go straight to http://www.google.com/analytics/. You will need to sign in using a gmail or gmail-enabled account and password. Follow the instructions; it will provide you with a few lines of computer code (Javascript) – which you don't need to understand – that you paste into every page of your website. Most website management programs – Web Content Management Systems in particular – offer you the option to paste it into one place so that it automatically propagates across every page.

From the moment you have installed Google Analytics, it begins to gather data about the behavior of visitors to your website. As each page is viewed by someone, that snippet of code you added sends a small set of data up to one of Google's servers. After only a few days, you can begin to see exciting reports. Google has done a fine job of making it user-friendly, so I would recommend just browsing through the reports one by one to see what is of most interest to you. You can add other users so that they can also view reports. After some weeks of use, you will find this piece of software an indispensable tool and you will wonder how you ever did without the kind of information it provides.

16: Posting new content at the same time every day

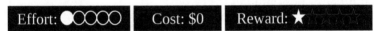

The more often you post new content to your website, the more frequently search engines will return to examine your website for new content. Let's assume for the moment that you are indeed posting new content every day and Google has caught up and is now also checking your website every day. This is not *certain*, but it is no harm to assume that it probably checks back at approximately the same time every day. Let's say, for example, that time of the day is 2pm. If you add your new content on a Monday at 9am, Tuesday at 5pm, and Wednesday again at 9am, this is how Google may see it: when it returns on Tuesday at 2pm, it will see that there is no new content since it last checked your website a day earlier. When it comes back – if it comes back – on Wednesday at 2pm, it will see that yes, there is new content, but that content is seen as one new addition, even though you added content two days in a row.

Solve this problem by adding your content every day at the same time. If your Web Content Management System allows you to schedule the time of the day that a given posting is to get published on the website, use it to publish at the same time every day. So, even if you post your new blog article some time during the day, consider setting the time of publication to 6pm. I say 6pm because it is likely close to your end of day. There is no need to publish at 4am – potentially a half day after you leave the office – and whether you write your article at 9am or 5pm, it will appear to search engines that your website publishes new content every day.

17: Naming image files using keywords

Effort: ●●○○○ | Cost: $0 | Reward★★★

Usually invisible to the person browsing a website, the actual name of image files is another way search engines match search words with page content.

I just Google'd the word *bicycle* on their image page and of the first sixteen images that displayed, thirteen of them contained the word *bicycle*. Yes, this is in image search and it is natural to assume a search engine would display image files containing the search word entered, but for text search image file names also play a role. This works in two ways: (1) the names of the images on a web page contribute to the keyword strength of those words on that page and (2) people searching for images often continue to the website where the search engine found the image. For example, if you sell high end competitive bicycles nationally, someone might search in Google images using the word *colnago* (a famous brand of Italian competitive bicycle), see the image colnago-bicycle.jpg on your website, then follow the link from the image to your website.

Can you tell what kind of content might be found on the websites containing these two images?
(a) *image405-ff-2011-x.jpg* and
(b) *24-hr-manhattan-vacuum-repairs.jpg*

> Instead of naming images esoterically – for example *3045a-2011.jpg* or *image5000a.gif* – name them with keywords from the web page they reside on. Where possible, use a variety of your keywords on different pages. This is an easy way to reinforce ownership of keywords across your website and it increases the likelihood of generating traffic from people doing image searches.

18: Populating image 'alt' text with keywords

Effort:    Cost: $0   Reward

Most images displayed on a web page are done using what is called the *img* tag.

Unfortunately, most Web Content Management Systems don't automatically populate this field with information.

If your Web Content Management System supports the addition of img *alt* text for each image that is uploaded to your website, consider something like this:

For each image, come up with a piece of text that will both help identify the contents of the image and support the keywords you are using on the web page that contains it. For example, suppose your website is for a business that offers bicycle sales, maintenance, service and repair in the lower manahattan. On your Service page, you have an image of you servicing an actual customer's bicycle. In this case, the alt text for that image might look like this:

<img src=".....manhattan-bicycle-service.jpg" alt="**customer's colnago bicycle being serviced at our 24-hr Manhattan service center**">

Alt text doesn't have to be short, either. Search engines will probably read at least the first one hundred characters, giving you plenty of space to include a half dozen or more keywords.

19: Populating image 'title' text with keywords

Effort: ●○○○○ | Cost: $0 | Reward: ★★

Just like the *alt* property of images, the *title* property gives you another opportunity to tell search engines what is contained in an image and elsewhere on the page that contains it.

For each image on each web page, include a value for the *title* property that contains your keywords from the web page. This can contain the exact same text as you populated in the image's *alt* property, in the previous action item. Here is an example of how it might look in the HTML:

```
<img src="…..manhattan-bicycle-service.jpg"
alt="customer's colnago bicycle being serviced at our 24-
hr Manhattan service center" title="customer's colnago
bicycle being serviced at our 24-hr Manhattan service
center">
```

In that one piece of text, you have included the name of a bicycle brand you service (Colnago), your primary location (Manhattan), and the keywords *service* and *bicycle*.

20: Using text or numbers instead of images

Many websites do indeed contain keywords, but are actually text in images. To the human eye, it may make no difference whether a product name is embedded in an image, but search engines cannot read them. Let's look at an example:

Which of the following pieces of HTML tells you what service is on offer on the website:

```
<img src="www.mycompany.com/servicebar.jpg">
```

or...

```
<h3>Bicycle Rental and Repair, Kirkland,
Washington</h3>
```

Both may look identical on a web page, but the latter is readable by search engines; the former is not.

In addition, the text version loads much faster in a browser, and may also appear in search results under the link to the page it contains.

Another common mistake is to embed telephone numbers in images. People who search for what you do may see your web page listed in search results, but may call a competing business because *their phone number* appears in search results. If your business's phone number is embedded in an image, it will not appear in search results. Often, people prefer to call a toll-free number that appears in search results rather than visit a website that is listed.

21: Adding your phone number to descriptions

As we touched on in the previous action item, certain businesses benefit from having their telephone number (or toll-free number) appear in search results, offering potential customers the option to call you without even visiting your website.

What types of businesses benefit most from this? Emergency services like plumbing, roofing, car towing, etc., benefit from it. Often, your potential customer is using a so-called "smart phone", and when they Google *car towing atlanta*, they simply call the first telephone number that appears in the list of search results. In fact, these new phones allow your potential customer to click the phone number and the phone calls you without the user having to type in your number. A pizza home delivery business may fit into this category too – certainly, my teenage kids think it fits into the category of emergency services – so having your telephone number at the beginning of the following fields may generate more sales, but may actually *decrease* the number of visitors to your website, because some of these new customers never visit your website.

Let's look at an example in the HTML code of a web page that adds their telephone number in the optimal way:

```
<meta name="description" content="1-800-555-1234
Emergency towing services of Seattle" />
```

When a person searches the Web for the type of product or service you offer, your web page may appear in the list of results because the page title, a heading or some text in the body of the page matches the search words the person entered, but the search engine may display what is called the meta description in search results, just like in the above example.

To begin with, look at your own home page. Click the *View/Source* (or *View/Page source*, depending on what browser you are using), then search for the text *meta name* until you find the description similar to that in the example. Does it contain your telephone number at the beginning?

Consider putting your telephone number or toll-free number at the beginning of the meta description for every page on your website that you believe has a chance of appearing in search results.

Your Web Content Management System may offer you the option to prefix every page's meta description with a fixed piece of text. If so, use it to prefix every page with your phone number.

Here is the result of a quick test I did. I Google'd the words *emergency towing services* and looked at the search results displayed by Google (see Illustration 11). One of the ads had a telephone number and one of the organic search results had a 1-800 number. I clicked that link to visit the web page and took a look at the source code for the page (using the *View/Page* Source menu item when the page was displayed).

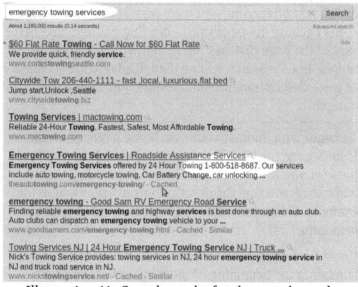

Illustration 11: Search results for the search words "emergency towing services"

```
<meta name="description" content="Emergency Towing Services
offered by 24 Hour Towing 1-800-518-8687. Our services include
auto towing, motorcycle towing, Car Battery Change, car
unlocking and more" />
```

Illustration 12: A piece of the source code for the web page offering "emergency towing services"

22: Populating the meta keywords field

Effort: ●○○○○	Cost: $0	Reward: ★★★☆☆

Every page on your website can have a field – the *meta keywords* field – that holds the seven best keywords for that page. Some say that the meta keywords field is no longer considered important, but I have not seen evidence to support that claim. In any case, it certainly does not hurt to populate this field. It is easy and free.

In the example in the box below, three fields (*title, meta description* and *meta keywords*) from a blog posting on kirklandcycle.com are shown. The one we are really interested in is the third of the three, the *meta keywords*, but all three are shown here to illustrate context. You will see how the *meta keywords* were loosely taken from the *meta description*, and how the page title was prefixed with the *meta keywords*.

<title>diabetes, exercise, cycling, bicycle, kirkland, sugar level, carbohydrates:: Bicycling and Type I Diabetes</title>

   <meta name="**description**" content="The 29-year-old learned at early age to gain control over his disease and gain quality of life despite dire predictions. Now he teaches what he knows to others through his competitive cycling team." />

<meta name="**keywords**" content="**diabetes, exercise, cycling, bicycle, kirkland, sugar level, carbohydrates**" />

The meta keywords are the seven words or terms most highly associated with the contents of the page. Note that a "keyword" can actually be two or more words (e.g. "sugar level" is considered one keyword). Keywords are separated by commas to help search engines know what words belong together (e.g. there is no comma between "sugar" and "level").

Note 1: the optimal number of keywords contained in the meta keywords field is *seven*.

Note 2: if keywords are not separated by commas, search engines may either take each word as a single keyword or regard the entire *meta keywords* field to be a single keyword.

23: Using keywords in page names

Effort: ●●○○○   Cost: $0   Reward: ★★★★☆

The name of a web page is one of the most important places search engines look for keywords to match search words.

What can you learn about the likely content of each of the following web pages?

.../career-counseling-services-lower-manhattan.html

and

.../page5000a-2011-12-15_testpage-publish.html

Clearly, the former tells us a lot, and search engines are no different. When they examine a page on the Web, the name of the actual page contributes enormously to the likelihood that a given search will match a search using those same words.

Take a look at your own website and see if the page names reflect the content of the page you are looking at.

Most modern Web Content Management Systems (WCM) today offer you the ability both to automate the creating of page based on words in the page title and to enter your preferred page name, overriding the one suggested by the WCM. For example, if you entered the page title *Bicycle Rentals and Repairs in Seattle*, your WCM might create your new page as *bicycle-rentals-repair-seattle.html*, which is far more search engine friendly than something like *page5049.html*.

24: Keeping page names static

Effort: ●●○○○ Cost: $0 Reward: ★★★

You probably know that search engines don't scan your entire website – or even parts of it – every day. At least, for most websites, that is the case. Neither do they scan the entire Internet every time someone does a search. Sorry if that sounds obvious – which it is of course – I just want to draw your attention to the fact that search engines match search words with the contents of your website the way it appeared at *some time in the past*. It might be comparing search words with how your website looked *yesterday,* or perhaps months ago. In addition, it might have looked at some of your web pages yesterday, and other pages weeks or months ago.

This means that, if yesterday you deleted (or renamed) a page that a search engine scanned three weeks ago, it may still offer that non-existent page to someone doing a search, even though a page with that name no longer exists on your website. If the searching person clicks the link to your web page, they may get a *Page not Found* error message.

At the time of new page creation, take the time to name it the way you want it to look forever. You can change the page name later, but be aware that search engines might believe for some time that the page still exists with the old name, unless you add a *Permanent 301 Redirect.* If you really must change a page name – for example, in the case of a product or company name change – you can add a *Permanent 301 Redirect* to point the old page name to the new page name. This will tell browsers and search engines that the old page name is now the new page name, and will take the visitor directly to the new page. See the Glossary entry for *Permanent 301 Redirect* on page 212 for details on how to do that.

25: Keeping pages forever

Effort: ●●○○○ Cost: $0 Reward: ★★★★

Content is to a website the way trees are to a forest. The more content you have the more website you have. In addition, old web pages on an active website can attract a qualitatively superior class of search engine traffic. Here's why:

A web page that contains something useful – for example, a blog post containing *My Grandmother's Seven Secrets for Staying Slim* – is an example of a potentially interesting and valuable piece of content that people may over time make links to. How does that happen? One example is what I talked about on page 40. People are always looking for interesting information to link to from their latest blog entry. The longer that piece of valuable content is available on the Internet, the more links to it will appear. And the more links to it that appear, the higher the *search engine stickiness* it achieves. Assuming its content value does not erode with time – as, for instance, a review of the latest iPod might do, because it is out of date quickly – keeping valuable old pages on your website can contribute greatly to the overall search engine stickiness of your website over time.

Some Web Content Management Systems allow you to keep web pages available to search engines yet not expose them through direct, visitor-visible links within your website. If your website is likely to grow substantially in numbers of pages – think dozens of new pages per day – it might make more sense to use such a feature. Examples of such websites might include newspapers and product sales websites with very large numbers of SKUs (Stock Keeping Units).

26:Making it easy for others to link to your site

You have probably seen this feature on other websites you have visited. It is a small toolbar (shown at the top of Illustration 13) that, when clicked, offers you a list of community websites in which you can add a link to this page.

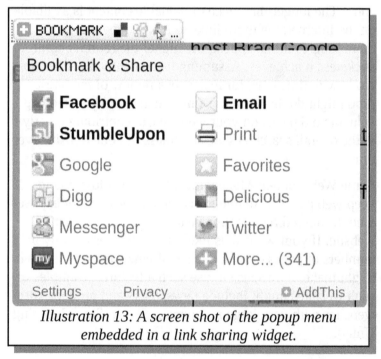

Illustration 13: A screen shot of the popup menu embedded in a link sharing widget.

There are several providers on the web that give you the button to add to your website completely free of charge. Two such providers are:

> www.sharethis.com and
>
> www.addthis.com
>
> Visit either site, enter your details and copy the HTML code it gives you, and add it to your web page. After you have done that (using whatever program you use to edit the contents of your website), the button will appear on that page on the Web.
>
> It's free and it's easy.

27: Reciprocal linking

If you've had a website for a while, you've probably by now received one or more emails from strangers inviting you to "swap links", or words to that effect. Their intention is to benefit from search engines' favoring of websites that have many links pointing to them. What harm, you might ask, is there if two websites simply help each other out in this way?

A rule-of-thumb I use for anything we do to improve our chances on the Web is to ask *where is the value to the website visitor*? And with a random link from an unrelated website, I'd have to say there was no visitor value, so I would be inclined not to bother with such link swapping.

If the site you are swapping links with is related to what you also do on *your* website, however, I might say Yes, there is potential value to a visitor on either of those websites. For example, if our example website kirklandcycle.com sold and serviced the *Colnago* brand of competitive bicycle, both the *Colnago* website and the Kirkland Cycle website would reasonably have a link to each other's website. Colnago might have it on their page that lists distributors in the Pacific Northwest of the US, and Kirkland might have a link to Colnago's website under a section labeled *More Information from the Manufacturer*, so clearly in that case, reciprocal links add value to the experience of visitors to each site.

Consider working with your business partners to create a link from your site to theirs and from their site to yours. This symbiosis reinforces the ownership of industry related keywords on each site.

Avoid creating reciprocal links just for the sake of increasing the count of links to your website.

28: Feeding the pages that work

Effort: ●○○○○	Cost: $0	Reward: ★★★☆☆

When I was converting a client's website a few years ago, my client wanted to delete the eighty press releases from the old website and not convert them to the new. I convinced them that those press releases were potentially valuable public content and could provide a great head start for content in the new website. So we did in fact convert all eighty of them to the new website. For each press release, I made note of any persons, product names, companies or any other likely keywords and placed them in the *page name, title, description* and *meta keywords* tag on each page, as well as in the body of the press release itself on each page. For most paragraphs, I created a few level 2 headers (using *header tags*). It just happened that within a day of switching to the new website, Google indexed the website from top to bottom. Almost overnight, traffic to the website went from about twenty a day to about eighty a day. What was most interesting, however, was that almost all of the extra traffic was going to two of the eighty press releases. Why? Because people were searching for whatever was on those pages.

Even with the best of planning, you can't know what pages will be the most popular until you see the visitors arriving. The eighty press releases gave us an opportunity to try a lot of different combinations of keywords relating to what the company was doing. We knew the press releases contained relevant content because, well, they were the company's press releases. We just didn't know which of the eighty – if any – would be popular in search.

How do you know which pages of your website are the most visited? Google Analytics (see page 57 for more about it) gives an excellent report, for any date range you select, of which pages are the most visited. It lists each page in order of most visited to least visited. See Illustration 14 to see how to view the most popular web pages on your website.

How do you "feed" your most popular web pages? Add more content to them. You know the existing content is working – because it has the most traffic – so you should just add a paragraph or two to the end of the body of text in each of the web pages that appear at the top of the report.

It so happens that this afternoon I was speaking with one of my clients. He asked me, *how could he tell which of his web pages were the most popular?* We went to Google Analytics and looked at his most popular report and nine out of the most popular ten pages of his website were pages on his blog. No surprise there.

*Illustration 14: To see the most popular pages on your website, from the Google Analytics Dashboard, click **Content** and **Top Content***

	Page None ⌄	Pageviews ↓
1.	/	3,019
2.	/bm/clients/add-product.shtml	673
3.	/index.shtml	648
4.	/bm/big-medium-training/how-to-	341
5.	/bm/about-us/index.shtml	326
6.	/bm/services/index.shtml	292

Illustration 15: A small snippet of the Google Analytics **Top Content** *report showing the most popular web pages on a single website. (The first row in the report reflects views of the Home Page of the site).*

29: Using header tags to promote most important keywords

Effort: ●○○○○   Cost: $0   Reward: ★★★

First, a primer on how Styles are used on websites.

Are you familiar with the concept of Styles in a word processor like Microsoft Word? In a nutshell, it's a way of controlling in one place the appearance of similar pieces of text throughout a document. For example, in this document I am typing, I have a style to control all chapter headers. If

I want to change the font for chapter headers to **bold**, I just change the Chapter style to bold, and all the chapter headers change to bold automatically.

Well built websites also use styles to control the appearance of text across all pages of the website. Just like in a word processing document, on a web site you also use styles to control the appearance of all pages. For example, if you wanted the main header on each page to be *dark green, 18-point font,* you set those properties in what is called the *Style Sheet* for the website; then you simply tag the piece of text on your page with 'h1' so the browser knows how to display it. Inside the page, it might look like this:

What it looks like in HTML (inside the web page)

<h1>Wild Flowers of Arizona**</h1>**

The **<h1>** tells the browser that *header level 1 begins here.* The **</h2>** tells the browser that *header level 1 ends here.* The marker to identify the header text above is called a *Header Tag.* On the *Style Sheet,* which is often in the same location as the home page and is usually called something like *mystyles.css,* the appearance of the header tag (header level 1 in this case) might look like this:

What it looks like (inside the Style Sheet for the website)

```
.h1
  {
     font-family: arial;
     font-weight: bold;
     font-size: 18pt;
```

```
   color: darkgreen;
}
```

You can have different levels of headers: h1, h2, h3, h4, etc..

If you've grasped what I have just described, you know how Style Sheets work; at least, enough to optimize the headers in your website for search engines.

When search engines examine a web page on your website, they give extra weight to text found between header tags. In our example below – which identifies a level 3 header – the word *Arizona* between the header tags might be given *three times* the weight of the same word appearing in the normal body text of the web page.

```
<h3>Wild Flowers of Arizona</h3>
```

This presents us with an opportunity to "add more weight" to our most important keywords in a page on our website. For your own website, take advantage of it by using header tags to identify headers on every page. If your website is already set up to use style sheets, this will be easy to do and will contribute to your web pages appearing higher up in search results.

30: Choosing the right time of the day and week to blog

Effort: ●●○○○	Cost: $0	Reward: ★★☆☆☆

When you are posting to any online community (e.g. Facebook, Twitter, StumbleUpon, etc.) or your own blog, be aware of the times of the day that your audience is most likely to respond positively.

Tuesdays and Thursdays are the days that people most often respond positively to an invitation to engage; that is, an invitation from you for them to become a lead by giving you their contact details.

People are happier later in the morning than when they have just woken up. They also respond more positively to business opportunities in the first half of the day and personal opportunities later in the day. On Friday afternoons, people might be more likely to connect with your story if it is to do with golf or weekend getaways.

Be aware of what time zone your target market lives in. In my Facebook account, for example, my business contacts tend to be on the west coast of the United States and my personal contacts tend to be in Western Europe, nine hours ahead. When I want my business contacts to see a Facebook posting, I will make sure I do it when people on the west coast are likely to be all awake, so that my post does not get covered by other posts (from different time zones) by the time the west coasters wake up and read it.

31: Separating the newcomers from those who know your website

Effort: ●○○○○	Cost: $0	Reward: ★★☆☆☆

When people look at website traffic reports, they are often looking at a mix of (a) visitors who found the website by searching for a solution like that offered on the website and (b) visitors who already know the company and simply searched for the company itself.

For the purposes of attracting more traffic to our website, we are less interested in those who already know our business and simply visit our website, and *more* interested in seeing how many people are finding us for the very first time. That is what organic search results are all about: *attracting new visitors*.

So how do we know which of the visitors are the ones that found us by looking for a solution to a problem?

In Google Analytics, the *keywords* report under *Traffic Sources* allows you to filter out all those search visitors who entered your domain name to find you. Let's say your company name is Light Matters and your domain name is www.lmatters.com. To exclude from the reports all those visitors who already know your company, you would change the report setting to *Exclude: matter*. That will exclude any searches that people made that had the word *matter* in them. So, whether they searched for the domain name (*www.lmatters.com*), part of the domain name (*matters.com*) or the company name (*Light Matters*), their search is excluded from the report, and we can narrow the report's focus to the visitors who found us for the first time.

Illustration 16 shows how to exclude from your Google Analytics reports those visitors who already know who you are.

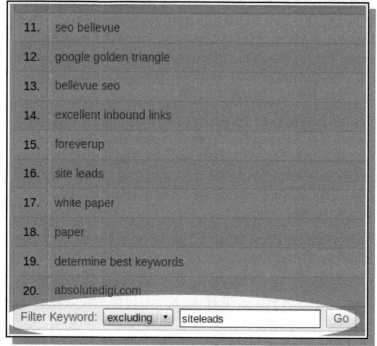

Illustration 16: "siteleads" was excluded from the web traffic report so that people who already knew the website or company would not be included in the report.

32: Train for a marathon, not a sprint

Building your engine to drive traffic to your website takes time.

One calm December morning many years ago, I was sitting on my couch by a window in my home in Seattle. My seven year-old son asked me, *Dad, do you think we're going to be able to make a snowman today*? I peered briefly out the window and, although there had been a mention of possible snow in the forecast the previous day, I responded to my son's inquiry with *there's probably a one-out-of-ten chance, son.* An hour or so later, I noticed a single snowflake falling from the sky. *Hey son,* I called to him, *your chances of making a snowman later today went from ten percent to maybe ninety percent.*

If you were to open a physical store in a busy shopping mall, walk-in traffic and sales would probably begin the day you opened your store for business. On the Web, unless you have a substantial budget for advertising, it will take time before the cash register rings on your website. The good news is, when it does begin, you are at the opening stages of what is called the *long tail effect*. Without going into a scientific explanation of how the *long tail effect* works, suffice it to say that once it begins to show results, it can go on for many years. In the case of your own web presence, once you see that first sale coming in, you know that – just like that first snowflake increases the chances that building a snowman will be possible – your first sale on the Internet is a very good sign of what is to come.

Two things are at play here. The first sale you make on your website shows that many elements are in the right place. You know strangers can find you, at least one person liked what they saw on your website, and at least one person was willing and able to make a purchase.

On the Web, it can take time to get to that first sale, when you are relying on organic search to deliver visitors. But when it does begin, you know you have answered a lot of questions about what pieces must be in place for it all to work. Assuming it is not a wild coincidence that that one person somehow stumbled into your website and mistakenly bought your product, it is now a question of doing more of what you have been doing to get that first sale. You improve, expand and optimize from here.

33: Blogging on your own domain

Effort: ●●●○○	Cost: $0	Reward: ★★★☆☆

If you are building a blog for the first time, consider housing the blog directly inside your website, assuming you own the domain name for your website.

For example, if your website were www.sboseries.com, your blog might be www.sboseries.com/blog. That is what is meant by having your blog inside your website.

Many websites have their blog elsewhere. For example, if your website were www.sboseries.com and your blog were sboseries.blogspot.com, it would mean that your blog actually resides on someone else's domain. There are two problems with that. One, the owners of the domain blogspot.com effectively own the content contained in your blog because your blog resides in a subdomain (sboseries.blogspot.com) of their domain (blogspot.com). They can do what they wish with your blog, including displaying ads or other material of their choosing. Secondly, your actual website is not getting the full value of the content investment you are making in your blog. If it did, you could have significantly more *search engine stickiness* on your main website because of the combined content value of both your website and blog acting as a single unit.

If you are planning on building a new blog from scratch, talk to your webmaster and/or website solution company and ask them if your new blog can be built inside the website as, essentially, a new directory within the existing website.

If you are building both a new website and a new blog, consider using a Web Content Management System that supports blogging within the website it creates.

34: Distributing White Papers across the Internet

Effort: ●●○○○ Cost: $0 Reward: ★★★

A White Paper is a document prepared by a company, individual or organization for a target audience, and speaks to a single topic and is presented from a single point-of-view. It is usually self-serving – which readers generally understand – and is a tried and tested method of "soft marketing" a product or service to potential customers by making an indirect but convincing argument to use the organization's product or service over others'. An example of a White Paper title might be *Reflexology and its Benefits to the Immune System*. Another might be *Using Business Intelligence to Support the Corporate Decision Making Process*. Inside the document, an argument is built up and concludes with the claim that *product such-and-such is the best solution on the market,* and so on. It is often used as a tool to help an evangelist for your product, working inside a customer organization, sell your product or service. The White Paper helps that evangelist convince his colleagues to close the deal.

There are websites that comb the Internet looking for White Papers to scoop up and post to their own websites. www.whitepapercentral.com is one such website. People go there to look for nicely presented, succinct documents to help them understand something or to move an issue forward within their own organization. Such White Paper repositories are a great place for you to get the word out about your product or service. For example, suppose you owned a company that sold care packages for people suffering from cancer. You might write a White Paper titled *Twelve Ways to Support a Loved One Through Cancer,* and post it to a White Paper repository. Inside the document, which is normally in PDF format, page headers and footers each contain a link or links back to pages on your website. When you are writing your own White Paper, any references in the document to, or images of, your actual products or services can be hot-linked back to your website. A product image may be linked directly to the Target Landing Page for that actual product on your own website.

It takes a reasonably good quality of writing and content for such a document to make its way to the top of the White Paper repository's search results, and for people to be interested enough to download it and read it, but it helps you in several ways:

1. Other organizations and individuals copy it and post it to their website, proliferating your message beyond the first repository.

2. Links from within the White Paper add to your own website's search engine stickiness.

3. People click the links from within your White Paper and follow them to your website, potentially increasing traffic to it.

There is serious competition for the top slots in any established White Paper repository, but if you already have good material that could become a White Paper, it might be easy enough for you to take advantage of this cost-free method of marketing.

Visit White Paper Central (www.whitepapercentral.com) and select one of the first documents on their home page. Examine it for clues to how a successful one might appear. Create your own, adding backlinks to it, and submit it to White Paper Central.

35: Cross referencing blog postings

Effort: ●○○○○	Cost: $0	Reward: ★★☆☆☆

If a person reads your blog posting *Seven ways to increase your chances of a promotion*, they may click a link to your blog posting *How to get a salary increase without really trying*. The longer you keep your visitor's attention, the more time you have to convert them into a lead. Each page they visit can be another opportunity to secure their contact information.

> As you write every new blog post on your website, consider which other blog posts – within the same blog of course – you could link to from the one you are writing.

Some people claim that links within a website count towards your total number of backlinks as considered by search engines, but I have not seen evidence to support that claim. The real reason for making it easy for visitors to step from one of your blog posts to the next is to keep their attention. The more time they invest in reading your website, the more likely they will surrender their contact information to you.

36: Creating a Site Map for your website

Effort: ●●○○○	Cost: $0	Reward: ★★☆☆☆

A Site Map serves two purposes, one of which we are more interested in. One, it provides visitors to your website an easy way to see how your website is laid out, especially if you have a website the structure of which is not entirely visible by simply moving a mouse over its navigation bar. Secondly, it provides to search engines a quick view of what pages exist on the website.

Some Web Content Management Systems (WCM) automatically create a Site Map for your website. Check with your webmaster and/or web solution provider to find out if yours does or does not. If it does not, you can create your own very easily, without any technical knowledge, and paste it into a page on your website.

Here is one way to add a Site Map to your website:

1. Visit www.xml-sitemaps.com and follow the instructions. Select the "HTML sitemap".

2. Copy the *HTML sitemap* and paste it into a new page on your own website.

3. Create a link from your home page – in the footer might be good place – and the job's done.

The XML Sitemap service does offer a "get it into Google" feature for you for a small fee, but it is easy to add the provided Site Map directly to your website.

More important than offering an easy way for visitors to view your website structure from a high level, is how easy a Site Map makes it for search engines to know where all the pages are in your website. Instead of Google – or any other search engine – having to scan your entire website to find all the links back and forth before it works out what all the pages are, a pre-built Site Map allows them to know what all the pages are from looking at a single page.

In addition, Google offers the feature where you can input the file name of your Site Map and it will scan that one file to see if any new pages have arrived. When you make it easy on the Google indexing process like this, it will be more likely to scan your website more often and more effectively.

Submitting your Site Map to the Google search engine:

1. Visit www.google.com/webmasters/tools/

2. Log in using the same account and password you used to view your Google Analytics reports

3. Click *Add a Site*

4. Enter the URL of the website you would like to add a Site Map for

5. Instructions vary based on where you host your website, but are clearly spelled out by this Google website.

37: Page strategy versus website strategy

Effort: ●●○○○   Cost: $0   Reward: ★★★

Have you noticed how search results are a list of web *pages*, not *websites*? Have you noticed that Google's term for quality is *Page*Rank not *Website*Rank? That is because the web page is the atomic unit of search and Search Engine Optimization (SEO). Even within one website, there can be a big difference in PageRank. Your home page could have a PageRank of 5, while a blog posting page on the same website may have a PageRank of 0. There are many reasons for such a difference, but for our purposes here, the important point to remember is to focus your traffic generation on specific web pages.

How does this affect your project to generate traffic for your website?

1. When you make a posting elsewhere on the Web, and you include a backlink to your own website, that link should point to a page on your website that best matches the keywords the external posting is trying to reinforce. For example, if you are talking on Facebook about a new lighting fixture product you are selling on your website, the link should point back to the product page dedicated to that lighting fixture.

2. When constructing a page on your website that you hope will attract *organic search results* traffic, think of the page in terms of solving a specific problem – and therefore a specific type of search – that your target visitor is trying to solve. When a person Googles *bike repair seattle*, the page they land on should reflect a solution to the problem the search person has. Having the page dedicated to the problem they are trying to solve increases the *search engine stickiness* for the search words and increases the chance the person will convert to a lead after they have arrived at the site.

38: Google Places: Adding your business

Effort: ●●○○○	Cost: $0	Reward: ★★★☆☆

Google, Microsoft, Yahoo and other search engines each have a feature to support businesses whose customers are local. By "local" I mean within driving or walking distance. If your customers are willing to drive or walk to you to buy what you have, they are *local*, and signing up for each of these search engines' local feature is something you can benefit from.

Local can be different for each business. If you run a Ford dealership in Tacoma, Washington, your customers may drive fifty miles to make a purchase. If you own a café across the road from that same dealership, your customers might all live within walking distance.

Illustration 17 On page 93 highlights the results of searching for a local plumber. Getting your business to appear in that short list under the ads – if any – can add significantly to the number of leads you generate from the Web. And you don't even need a website to use this free service offered by Google and other search engines.

Illustration 17: Google search results showing ads and Google Places. A business can add their own entry for Google Places and control what is displayed.

The Google pages you use to add your business to Google Places change quite frequently, so the screen shot may be a little out-of-date. Aside from your business's physical address, however, just two of the fields you will be asked to enter data for are important. They are *Business Name* and *Description*. That is because Google relies on these two fields more than any other to determine a good match between your business listing and search words used by people in your neighborhood looking for a product or service like yours.

How to add your business to Google Places:

1. Visit maps.google.com

2. Click *Put your business on Google Maps...*

3. Complete the required fields.

4. Once you have pressed Submit, a week or so later, you can expect a physical postcard to arrive in the mail with a code printed on it. With that postcard in hand, return to maps.google.com and click *Put you business on Google Maps* again. Enter the number printed on the card in the appropriate field and follow any remaining instructions.

I highly recommend reading the entire requirements page for adding an entry into Google Places. You will see it when you are asked to *accept the terms of the agreement* by checking a box on the screen. There are fairly strict rules about what is acceptable and what is not. For instance, they do not allow you to use PO boxes as your business address – so if you are using an apartment or condominium number, put for instance apt t-123 in your address to show it is clearly not a PO box – neither do they allow you to stuff keywords into your business name. These rules are likely to get a little stricter over time, as Google uncovers new and creative ways outsiders game the system. Still, a good *Business Name* will at least mention your city of operation, and a good *Business Description* will also mention it and the services you provide. Be honest and be thorough. For instance:

(Business name)
Driscoll Plumbing of Sammamish, WA

(Business Description)
Providing installation, maintenance and repair or water, gas and sewage piping in the Sammamish, Issaquah and

---

> *Redmond areas of Washington. We also repair and*
> *replace broken water heaters and bathroom fixtures.*

Both the business name and the business description
contain additional clues and keywords – without being
overstuffed with them – to help search engines match
location-specific searches match up with your business. A
location-specific search is one where the searching person
needs to find a business that is close to them. Search
engines know whether a search is location-specific or not
by examining the search words. For example, searching for
plumber lower manhattan will likely result in a list of
Google Places, but a search for *oscar wilde quotes* will not.
If your business's customers are within driving distance,
you definitely need to complete your entry in Google
Places. It's easy, it's free and it helps your customers find
you.

39: Google Places: Asking your customers to review your business

Effort: ●●○○○○   Cost: $0   Reward: ★★★

In the good old days, a diligent business owner would ask a
happy customer to tell their friends, or otherwise pass the
good word on to other potential customers. Today, many
people rely on reviews posted on Google Places and other
websites like Facebook, Twitter, Angie's List and many
other places. There are so many, it is hard to keep up.

The best thing anyone can do for their business of course is
to provide good products and good services. Still, getting
the good word out in all the new ways is becoming more

and more important. Google Places has a feature that allows your customers to say nice things (or not) about your business. You can see in Illustration 17 on page 93 that the number and quality of the reviews for each business listed is also shown. People are so used to seeing reviews (reflected by stars and/or numbers), they respond often by clicking the line with the best review rating.

When a customer expresses satisfaction with your product or service, invite them to post a review of your business on Google Places. You can do this by printing on the back of your business card something like that shown in Illustration 18 on page 96.

If you are happy with our service, please leave a review here: www.google.com/places

If you are unhappy, please call me at 206-555-1150

Illustration 18: Printed on the back of your business card, this makes it easy for your customers to create a positive review on Google Places, which in turn, appears in your Google Places listing.

40: Bing Local: Adding your business

Effort: ●●○○○   Cost: $0   Reward: ★★★☆☆

Microsoft Bing has a local listing feature that operates in a similar fashion to that of Google Places. It allows you to enter your business details, including physical location, and this information in turn may be displayed when people search for a product or service like yours. Bing displays local businesses in a similar way to how Google Places displays theirs.

It is worth noting that Bing popularity has increased somewhat since its arrival on the search engine scene. Even if it accounts for a fraction of the search activity enjoyed by Google, many businesses ignore it for that very reason, which means the competition for the top slots is less in *Bing Local* than it is in *Google Places*. So take advantage of it and add your business there too.

There is also a regional component to which search engines are preferred. I know from experience that in the Pacific Northwest of the United States, Microsoft Bing commands a higher percentage of overall usage than it does, for instance, in Silicon Valley in Northern California. It has a lot to do with the fact that Microsoft is around the corner and many of their employees, vendors and customers are greatly influenced by their proximity to Microsoft. Still, my recommendation is, if your customers are local – that is, if they are within driving distance of your business – take advantage of this free service provided by Microsoft and see if you can scoop up a few more leads.

Visit www.bingbusinessportal.com

1. Log in and follow the instructions to add your business to Bing Local listings.

2. When entering your business name, *Driscoll Plumbing of Sammamish* is superior to *Driscoll Plumbing*.

3. When entering your business description, mention your services and locations serviced.

4. Look at the call-out box on page 94 to see an example of a business name and business description that will help Bing Local match searches with your services and location.

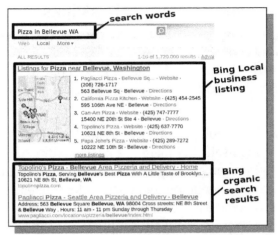

*Illustration 19: Microsoft Bing search results displayed for the search **Pizza in Bellevue WA**. Getting your business to appear in that first list of local business listings can make a significant difference to your lead generation success.*

I have not seen reviews appear yet within the Microsoft Bing Local business listings. I would be surprised if Microsoft doesn't get round to adding that functionality because in Google Places, it adds a significant amount of credibility beside a business listing if a person can see that other visitors have already independently critiqued each business. So look out for that feature in Bing Local, and be sure to encourage your satisfied customers to add a review for your business when they express satisfaction with your product or service.

41:Facebook: concurrent backlinks

Effort: ●●○○○	Cost: $0	Reward: ★★★★☆

We know that we should include a link to our website from every Facebook posting. But what about the other way around?

For every Facebook posting, add a link from your website to the posting itself. But there is a knack to this so that search engines can actually see your posting. Remember, search engines cannot log into Facebook accounts, so you have to provide the public link to the page. Here is an example: suppose one of your suppliers announced a new product and you wish to share a photo of it on your Facebook account. Once you have finished making the posting, you view the photo in your Facebook album. To see the public link – that is, the link visible to search engines – press F5 on your browser and the display will change to *normal view.* At the bottom of your screen, you will see a link below this text *Share this photo with anyone by sending them this public link:.* Copy that link to your Clipboard and use it to link from the corresponding product page back to Facebook. Remember to use Anchor text to support your keywords, including the brand name of the product you are talking about with this sharing on Facebook. To understand how Anchor text works, see page 51.

So, what has happened? You have reinforced ownership of those keywords within your Facebook account by pointing to it from a page on your website that uses those keywords heavily.

Here are the steps. This works also for visitors to your site who do not have an account on Facebook, as well as search engines:

1. Looking at the posting you just made to your Facebook account, click the time stamp below it (e.g. *53 minutes ago* or *June 11, 2012*, etc.)

2. In the address bar of your browser, you will see the direct link to the page. Copy it to the Clipboard.

3. Where you manage your own website, open the page for the product (or other page most closely related) you just talked about or shared on your Facebook account. Select or add text that describes the product. For example, *Prandina Recessed Ceiling Fan available at Light Matters*. Add the link you copied to your Clipboard a moment ago from all of that text.

42: Facebook: using your keywords in posts

Effort: ●●○○○   Cost: $0   Reward: ★★★

This might sound obvious, but using your keywords inside the Facebook posting helps.

If you are selling a product with high brand value – for example, Tiffany jewelry – consider the brand name of the product to be one of your keywords. Some 70% of large brand name companies fail to support their own brand name in Facebook, so the opportunity might be there for you to take advantage of.

Even when you share (using your Facebook account) someone else's Facebook posting, you get the opportunity to overwrite the default text header and summary paragraph. For example, you see a product launch page for the new Lenovo laptop and you decide to share it on your Facebook account. Before you click the final *Share Link* (or *Share Video* etc.) button, it allows you to change the text as it will appear to friends on your Facebook account. Does it contain keywords to support your keyword strategy? If not, change it to do so.

43: Facebook: A popularity contest

| Effort: ●●●○○ | Cost: $0 | Reward: ★★★★ |

Facebook is so big it is almost its own Internet. As far as search engines are concerned, your Facebook account is like a website in its own right. The count and quality of 'Likes' on your Facebook account is – roughly speaking – similar to the count of backlinks to your website, and we know that backlinks to your website are critically important. So too are 'Likes' to your Facebook account, and the more 'Likes' you have accumulated to your Facebook account, and the higher the quality of them, the higher up your Facebook pages will appear in search results.

Success on Facebook, therefore, consists of several factors, including (1) the *number* of 'Likes' you have accumulated and (2) the *frequency* of new content (3) the *quality* of new content and (4) the *regularity* of new content you add to your Facebook account. Yes, just when you thought you had the whole website scene licked, along comes a "new Internet" called Facebook.

Encourage your friends and contacts in Facebook to click the 'Like' for postings that you consider important and relevant to your business success.

44: Facebook: Adding a Fan Page

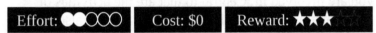

Effort: ●●○○○ | Cost: $0 | Reward: ★★★

A Facebook Fan Page enables you to focus highly relevant attention on a specific element of your business, or perhaps the business itself, and it serves as another means to gather the contact details of Web travelers who are interested in what your organization has to offer.

You might have a personal Facebook account for your friends, relatives and so on, but you can also have a Fan Page – for example – for your dog-walking business. Such a Fan Page would be a way of focusing dog-walking related conversations in your life into its own "forum" - that is, your Fan Page - while still keeping a loose connection back to your main Facebook account.

I have seen Fan Pages relating to rock stars, stamp collections, churches, politicians, environmental movements, school projects, products and all kinds of services. There's even one called *Moon Landing Hoax*, where people who believe the Apollo Moon landings were a staged fiction created by the US Government come together to prove it to anyone who is interested.

The advantage of having a Fan Page is that it creates a laser like focus on a specific subject – on a single page – versus a whole Facebook account which is used for a more general audience among friends and contacts.

Depending on the purpose of your Fan Page, the instructions for creating one are going to be a little different, but it is an easy step. For any Fan Page you create, the objective of the exercise is to publish to the world and gather interest in a product, service or activity you are involved in. Central to that are the activities of accumulating quality links to the Fan Page and also to increase the number of *Likes* to it. Both of these will increase your Fan Page's *search engine stickiness* and thus, will bring your message closer to the top of search results.

Create a Fan Page:

If the following link is inactive, you can Google *create a facebook fan page* to find the new location, but likely this will work or get redirected to the new location if it has been moved.
http://www.facebook.com/pages/create.php

Select the type of business or interest that applies to your business. Fill in the boxes and click save. Remember to use your best keywords in the page description.

After you have completed the addition, introduce the Fan Page to your friends to begin with, and link to it from elsewhere, including your website.

To find the direct link to your new Fan Page:

Go to your Facebook home page, under "Pages" on the left hand column – or the Fan Page itself if it is your sole Fan Page so far – click the name of your new Fan Page. The URL in the address bar, up to the character right before the '?', is the direct link to your Fan Page. Use that URL to create a link from your website to your new Fan Page whenever you refer to it, or include it in an email when you refer to your Fan Page.

45: YouTube: creating your first video

Effort: ●●●○○ | Cost: $0 | Reward: ★★★

YouTube offers another off-page means for people to learn about the product or service you offer and potentially become a future customer or client.

Did you know, YouTube is the second largest search engine in terms of how many searches are performed every day? It's hard to know what people are searching for, but there is a lot you can do to make sure your videos are are least visible when people search for what you do.

The reason these websites (Facebook, Twitter, YouTube, etc.) are so popular is because they are fresh and authentic. The price viewers pay for those qualities is that content is not perfect. In fact, viewers see imperfection as a signature of such content. Instead of the sanitized and scrubbed news playing out on structured television and radio, the Internet brings us directly in touch with the news maker. I'm telling you this because I don't want you to worry about quality for the moment. When you feel yourself stiffening up in front of the camera, remember that people don't expect you to be as polished and comfortable as Bill Maher is when his show is running.

Probably the biggest obstacle to exploiting the power of YouTube is – for most people – shooting the video in the first place, so this is how I help my clients get over that: Using a $100 dollar standard definition digital video camera, I point it at my client as if I were recording them, and simply ask them questions about their business. In one case, my client's camera had not arrived yet, so I used an unopened Cup Noodle pack as a fake camera. It added a little comic relief, which helped all of us relax and get the job done with a smile on our face. Once we passed the threshold "oh, I wish we had recorded that one", I knew it was time to use the real camera.

Tips on getting a simple, effective video clip:

- Practice first with the camera off or with a fake camera.

- Shoot for one question at a time. For example, *what service does Acme Rentals offer their clients*? You, the business owner, will answer the question, which will be the bulk of the clip duration.

- Be prepared to shoot each clip many times before you get one that is good enough.

- If you make a mistake in the middle of a clip, keep going to the end, even though you know you will not use that one. The start-to-finish is also an important element to practice.

- Keep each clip short. Usually sixty to ninety seconds is enough to begin with. You can do longer videos when you become more comfortable.

- Remove distractions from "the set" before you shoot. (In one video of a life coach on YouTube, the presenter's dog was "grooming" himself on a chair in the background; I found myself wondering what breed the dog was, and lost track of what the presenter was saying).

- If you have a video editing program on your computer, use it to clip the start and end of the video if there are any slack times, particularly if you shot the clip alone, where you can be seen walking from the camera to a chair, and then back again at the end of the clip to switch the camera off.

Even if you have a single, ninety-second video clip about your business offering, it may be enough. The more the merrier, of course, but once you have done one, doing more is a snap.

46: YouTube: Deciding on the content of the video

Effort: ●●●○○   Cost: $0   Reward: ★★★

There are videos on YouTube, created by teenagers, that have been viewed *millions* of times. I saw one the other day, in fact, that had been viewed forty-five million times. Now, it is challenging to get your video into the millions of views, but making your video compelling will encourage viewers to pass it to their friends and give it a thumbs-up on

YouTube. Illustration 20 on page 109 is a screen capture of a YouTube video that has had over a hundred thousand views. Approximately 96% of the viewers who voted using the *Like/Dislike* buttons voted with the *Like* button. A compelling video will have a much higher percentage of *Likes* versus *Dislikes*.

A compelling video relating to your business will offer value to the viewer. My preferred approach for adding value in a video (or a book like this one, for that matter) is to structure it into discrete "nuggets" or related information. For example, if your business was the construction of competitive bicycles, the video might be *Nine Easy Steps to Shortening Your Finish Time in Competitive Cycling*. In the video, I would run through the steps one by one, so that the viewer understands, at a high level, how they can act today on the advice contained in the video. This will increase their interest in watching the video in the first place, increase the likelihood they will pass the link to others, and increase the chances of their becoming a customer down the road (no pun intended).

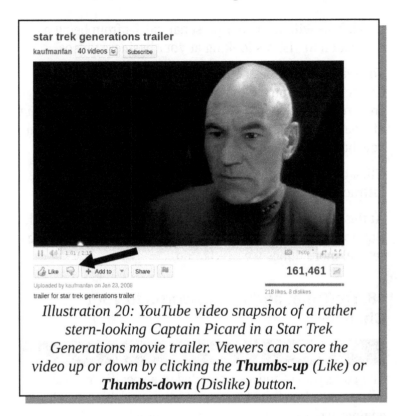

*Illustration 20: YouTube video snapshot of a rather stern-looking Captain Picard in a Star Trek Generations movie trailer. Viewers can score the video up or down by clicking the **Thumbs-up** (Like) or **Thumbs-down** (Dislike) button.*

47: YouTube: uploading your business video

So now, you have a video and it is time to upload it to YouTube. Ideally, set up an account on YouTube that is dedicated to your business, using your business name and so on. This will keep your personal videos from being a distraction to visitors looking at your business videos.

To create a YouTube account, click (who'd have guessed) Create Account on the top of the YouTube screen. (If you are already logged into your own personal account, sign out of YouTube first). Follow the instructions for creating your new business related account and sign into it.

Click the *Upload* link to upload your video and follow the instructions.

At this point, your first video is visible to the whole world! But, to increase the chances someone will find it, there are several more things we need to do...

48: YouTube: adding keywords to your Channel

Effort: ●●●○○   Cost: $0   Reward: ★★★☆☆

The collection of videos uploaded to a specific YouTube account is a YouTube Channel. Understandably, search engines have a tough time working out what a video actually contains, so we will add keywords to your Channel to solve that problem.

Click your logged-in name (at the time of writing this, it was situated near the top-right-hand-side of the YouTube screen). A menu will appear, and you will click *Videos*. Press *Edit* under any one of your videos. In the *tags* box, enter your best guess search words people are likely to use to find the product or service you offer. Click *save changes* when you have done that.

These changes may take some time to get picked up by search engines. The best thing you can do to increase your chances of generating traffic from these videos is to have plenty of them. Because they are all in the same YouTube Channel, when someone views one of them, that person is more likely to be presented with your other videos. If you do many videos, consider using a numbering system when naming your videos to show the viewer what order they are best viewed in. For example:

Life Coaching 1: Active Listening
Life Coaching 2: The Client Finds his/her own Answers
Life Coaching 3: Being non-judgmental

You probably know that Google now owns YouTube, and they apply the same rigorous rules to gaming the system as they do in *Google Search* and *Google Places*. And just as when you add content to YouTube, read the rules and avoid being blacklisted or getting your account suspended or deleted.

49:Donning a White Hat

Effort: ●●●○○   Cost: $0   Reward: ★★★

A good rule-of-thumb for deciding what to do or not to do with respect to generating traffic or generating leads is to ask yourself *Does this add value to the Web traveler's experience*? If the answer is Yes, then the action is quaintly referred to as *White Hat*, and it is likely a good thing to do in the long run. Success on this new Internet of ours is to a large part a question of adding value to others' experience in order to develop relationships.

On the other hand, you can ask yourself *Is what I am doing an attempt to trick search engines or visitors into visiting my website*? If the answer is Yes, then the activity is known as *Black Hat*.

An example of a White Hat activity is adding a new blog entry to your website every day. An example of a Black Hat activity is exchanging inbound links with websites that have nothing to do with your website and thus, do not add any value to the Web traveler's experience of your website.

Avoid Black Hat activity because in the long run, search engines wise up to it and any time, effort or money invested in it will have been wasted. And besides, you want to do the right thing to make the Web a valuable experience for all of us, right?

50: Using Google+ to help people find you

As of writing this, Google+ – Google's latest entry into the online community application world – is a few months old. Thus far, it appears to be a mix of Facebook, Twitter and then some. And if history is anything to go by, its functionality and power will grow quickly.

Google+ allows you to expose all of your Google+ content to search engines. It is probably also reasonable to expect Google to favor its content over that of Facebook, Twitter or any other such community. So, my recommendation at this point is to set your Google+ account to full exposure. You do that by adjusting the setting on your Google+

account. Under Settings / Profile and privacy, click the Edit visibility on profile, as shown in Illustration 21.

Illustration 21: In your Google+ account settings, click Profile and privacy to access the Profile Visibility screen.

Once on the visibility screen, shown in Illustration 22, check the *search visibility* option.

As of late 2011, Google is said to be most popular website on the Internet. Facebook is the second most popular. Google has been worried about the long term threat of Community websites in general and Facebook in particular, so it has come out with a string of attempts to turn back the Facebook tide, all of them flops – Orkut, Jaiku, Wave, Buzz – that had no chance of beating Facebook. But with Google+, they have a real chance to steal a substantial share of Facebook's membership. With their deep integration into all things Internet, Google only has to be as good as Facebook to create a huge distance between Google+ and Facebook. But that is just the start of it. It will likely become "its own Internet". If you haven't already done so, sign up for Google+, and sign up on www.sboseries.com for free updates to this book to cover Google+ as it emerges.

51: Buying ads versus organic search results

Bidding for ads in Google AdWords and elsewhere is a question of what profit you can expect from a given ad. If you are selling a small number of products, your average profit from a new customer might be – let's pick an example - $30. But you might be competing with a much larger company that also sells your products, but because they sell so many more products than you do, their average customer lifetime profit is $200. So, your competitor can afford to outspend you in advertising for what is essentially the same product.

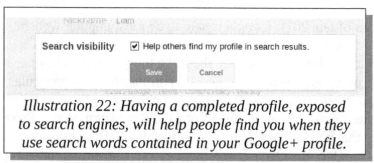

Illustration 22: Having a completed profile, exposed to search engines, will help people find you when they use search words contained in your Google+ profile.

What do you do? Rely on *organic search results*. At least, for your long keyword strategy. Use AdWords to bid for products you own than have a low competitive profile, and use all the organic search methods outlined in this book to get your website to appear at the top of organic search results.

A question people often ask me is, *how much should I spend on ads*? For most companies, ads are used to find new customers. And for each such new customer, there is profit to be gained. When you know how much you can expect to profit from a new customer – across the life time of that customer – you know your absolute budget in advertising for that one customer. Let's look at an example:

Your company designs, manufactures, markets and sells a range of toys – let's say fifty SKUs (Stock Keeping Units, or unique products). You sell some direct, and indirectly through several other organizations (for example Amazon.com, Toys R Us, etc.). Because you only have a limited number of products, your profit on a new customer will be substantially less than the profit on a new customer for Amazon.com, because they have hundreds of thousands of other products they can cross-sell to each new customer. Their new customer profit might be $100, while your new customer profit might be $15. This means a click-through for an ad they place is worth far more than a click-through from an ad you place.

What does that mean? It means, even though the products you and your competitors are selling are yours, you are unlikely to beat out bigger players with ads for the same product. That is why organic search is usually – but not always – a better choice of investment for companies selling nationally or globally.

> For small companies targeting a national or global market, and competing with big online companies, organic search is usually a better investment than online advertising.

For companies looking for *local* customers, however, online advertising can be very profitable.

> For small, local service companies – that is, when their customers are within driving distance – online advertising can be very beneficial.

Summary:

For most small companies competing nationally or globally, it is difficult to out-bid large companies for the same keywords because larger companies tend to make more money from each new customer they acquire. That means, they can bid a higher price for the same set of keywords than a small company can bid.

The advantage a small company has over a bigger company, however, is they usually find it easier to add fresh, useful content to their website – most likely in the form of a new blog posting every day – and thus may appear in organic search results while their big competitor appears in an ad on the same page.

In the long run, which is really all that matters in business, organic search results are superior to online advertising in several ways:

- The content attracts search traffic forever.

- The effect of new content on organic search results increases geometrically over time, if you continue to add content every day.

- Visitors regard organic results as superior to ads. Thus, a click-through visitor from organic search is worth more than a click-through visitor from an online ad. They are more likely to become a customer.

52: Latent Semantic Indexing

Effort: ●●○○○○   Cost: $0   Reward: ★★★

Google and other search engines regard a page as more valuable when keywords in the page title are supported by related words within the body text of the page itself. For example, if a page title is *Couch, Table and Chair Rentals in Lower Manhattan*, words or terms found in the page itself – like a*rmchair, closet, cupboard, bench,* and so on – reinforce the keywords in the page title.

Search engines perform what is called Latent Semantic Indexing, or LSI for short, on each page to determine how well the content of a page matches the page title in terms of related words, not the exact keywords repeated over and over.

Search engines do this to get around those website owners who simply stuff every field on their web pages with the same keywords, in an attempt to attract website visitors by gaming the search engines, without offering good value to the visitor.

Increasing website traffic without spending money

Stuffing a web page with a given set of keywords purely for the purpose of appearing higher up in search results is a Black Hat activity and search engines frown upon it. What's more, they have gotten very good at spotting such pages and reducing them in rank. Thus, we are back to the basic principle of *doing whatever enhances the experience of the website visitor*. In the long run, that is the only thing that matters.

Latent Semantic Indexing is your friend. It works to filter out those organizations on the Internet who make it their business to trick search engines. Pushing the tricksters to the side makes more room at the top of search results for you – who by now understands the value of honest, useful content – and rewards you for delivering good value to your prospects, customers and the world in general!

How to make LSI your friend:

1. Whoever adds content to your site, make sure they produce quality, valuable and original content.

2. Always ask yourself *will this content be interesting and valuable to the reader*?

3. If your page title is *How to repair a flat tire*, make sure the page content explains how to repair a flat tire.

4. Don't use software that generates content automatically.

5. Do not overuse keywords in your, for example, blog posting.

Spending a little money

53: Registering keyword-dedicated domain names

| Effort: ●●○○○ | Cost: $100 | Reward: ★★★☆☆ |

Have you ever noticed that certain searches result in a domain name containing those exact words appearing sometimes at the very top of search results? For example, you search for *kirkland bicycle rentals* and the first on the list of search results is a website with the URL www.kirkland-bicycle-rentals.com, a domain name made up of the exact search words you used. Often, such domain names will beat out websites that are otherwise far better candidates – you would think – for search results.

How can you know which keyword combinations would make good domain names to own? To answer the question takes a little experimentation. Most website owners – sooner or later – are puzzled when keywords they thought their website would score very high in don't bring them to the top of search results. Are there search words you know your potential customers are using but that don't result in your website appearing on page one of search results? Let's look at an example:

Imagine you owned a company that specialized in performance bicycle design and was called *Kirkland Cycle* (in Kirkland, WA). When you Google *performance bicycle design kirkland*, your website does not show up in search results. To solve this problem – or at least, increase your chances of appearing higher up in search results – you buy the domain name performancebicycledesignkirkland.com and/or performance-bicycle-design-kirkland.com, and make a simple, one-page website for each of the two domains. Each website becomes a *Target Landing Page* dedicated to attracting visitors who searched using the words *performance bicycle design kirkland*. Those exact search words are used – let's take a wild guess here – perhaps a hundred times a year. That's not a lot of searches, but you do score a potential bullseye when it does come up. For a hundred dollars (ten years of domain name ownership) it might well be worth it if you can scoop two customers a years from it, if each customer is worth several thousand dollars in profit to you.

We could have made the task a little easier for ourselves by simply pointing the new domain name – using a *Permanent 301 Redirect* – directly at our existing website, but we would have compromised the focus of those specific words in the domain name by not offering a domain name that contained those exact keywords. That is, if we had simply redirected the domain name at a page in our existing website, search engines take the keywords from the destination domain name, not the originating one. In addition, our current website might dilute the overall strength of these exact search words.

What we have done is create a highly search words-specific page on the Internet and turned it into a discrete, standalone *Target Landing Page* (TLP). On that TLP, we invite the new visitor to engage with us by way of special offer, as described on page 158.

At about ten dollars per domain name per year, this method of grabbing very specific combinations of keywords and converting a percentage of the visitors to leads may be very worthwhile.

> Before you spend any money on this little project though, do a little research on search words that result in your competitors appearing at the top of search results. There might be a handful of good candidates that pop out.
>
> Even though each domain name you do this for is only going to have a single page, make sure the *page title*, *page description*, *meta keywords*, the image names, *alt texts* and *titles* all use the very same keywords you used

in the domain name. All of it combines to make a laser-sharp focus on just those few search words, undiluted by any other less related words on your website.

54: Purchasing and redirecting a mature domain name

| Effort: ●●○○○ | Cost: $500 | Reward: ★★★ |

Search engines favor domain names that have been around for a long time over domain names that are younger.

How do you determine how old a domain name is? Visit www.internic.net, click the "Whois" link at the top of the web page, and enter your domain name (e.g. myspecialplace.com) and click the submit button. In a few moments, it will display a report. About thirteen lines below the submit button, you will see the *creation date*.

For most organizations, it is not possible to simply change their domain name to an old one, even if they already own the rights to an old one they could use. That is because the organization has invested heavily in the brand value of their current domain name, even if it is for six months in the early stages of a startup or online store, the cost of changing the domain name is often prohibitive. It is not just the investment in brand, but it is also email addresses, logo design, and dozens of other investments. How do you get around that? You do what is called a *Permanent 301 Redirect* to point the old domain to the new domain, and leaving the newer domain name functioning exactly as it is.

It doesn't matter much what the domain name is, as long as its creation date is years in the past; ten years is very good, twelve or more years is excellent. It could be called gobbledygook.com. Its name is unimportant because no one will see the name. But its *age value* – in the view of search engines – will be credited to your newer domain name.

> You can buy old domain names in a number of places. One example is the *Auctions* section on godaddy.com. Give yourself a budget of about $500 and try to buy one that is ten or more years old, then point it to your nameservers, (It doesn't matter much whose nameservers you point it to, as long as you have enough authority to add a *Permanent 301 Redirect* from there to your existing domain name).

55: Extending the life of your domain name

Effort: ●○○○○   Cost: $50   Reward: ★★★

Domain names that are registered for years into the future are favored by search engines over domain names that will expire within the next year. There are two reasons for this. First, scam websites are usually only registered for a single year, probably because the scam is busted within only a few months. Secondly, a domain name that is registered years into the future is more likely to be around for longer, so search engines rightly regard it as a good candidate for showing earlier in search results.

The website for support of this book is www.sboseries.com, therefore its domain name is sboseries.com. In other words, the domain name for a given website is arrived at simply by removing the 'www' and the period right after it.

How do you find out how long your domain name is registered for? Visit www.internic.net and click the "Whois" button at the top of the page. Type in your domain name and press enter. In about ten seconds a report will be displayed. Look for the line that shows Expiration date:

Expiration Date: 20-mar-2017

The per-year cost of registering a domain varies between about seven and twenty dollars. I recommend to clients who are registering a brand new domain for the very first time to pay for at least five years, usually five or ten years to begin with.

How do you add more years to the registration of your domain name?

Contact whoever is hosting your website and ask them who the *Registrar* (see Glossary entry on page 213) is for your domain name. It is often the same organization that both hosts the website and is the *Registrar* for its domain name. Contact the Registrar through the website and ask them what the procedure is for extending the life of your domain name. The further into the future the better, but usually five years will be enough.

A website on a domain that is registered for years into the future is likely to display higher in search results than it would if the domain name is due to expire within less than a year.

56: Buying backlinks

Effort: ●●○○○ Cost: $100 Reward: ★☆☆☆☆

Because backlinks – or inbound links – to your website are believed to increase your website's *search engine stickiness*, businesses that create backlinks for you have sprouted up on the Web. For several hundred dollars, you can buy a few hundred supposedly high quality backlinks.

Creating backlinks is a time-consuming job, so it is no surprise to see the work being done in developing countries where hourly pay is much lower. For example, www.backlinksphilippines.com offers 400 backlinks for a hundred dollars.

The problem I have with it is that it usually offers no real value to visitors to your website. Secondly, Google and other established search engines have wised up to backlinks created in this way. Still, it is worth mentioning, because such backlink creation companies may be able to create the links on websites related to your business.

Spending more money: Google AdWords

I've served my time in big corporations – twelve years in Siemens and another five at Microsoft – and I've spent most of the fifteen years since then in startups. I've been asked the question more than once, *what is the difference between a startup and a corporation?* My answer is, *a startup is an experiment; a corporation is a set of processes.* And when I consider the challenge an existing company has in becoming successful on the Web, it looks more like that of a startup than it does a corporation. It feels a lot like an experiment. You try everything you can reasonably afford to try, until the evolving formula works.

Because there is potentially so much money involved, you might consider spending time to understand Google AdWords in depth before you buy any ads. I have found over the past decade that Google AdWords is sufficiently complex that it requires a degree of specialization and that – unlike lead generation based on organic search results – merely dabbling in it is likely to just cost money and offer little return. Still, I will share with you my experience in helping clients get started in Google AdWords, and also my direct experience in spending my own money on it.

If you wish to dig deeper, an excellent, 550-page reference manual called *Advanced Google AdWords* by Brad Geddes is a good place to start.

57: Not for beginners

Much as Google would like you to believe that AdWords are easy to be successful with, it is very easy to blow a lot of money on ads without even covering your costs. As an advertising executive put it, *advertising is easy when you don't have to sell anything*. Yes, you can be up and running, bidding for AdWord placements, and you will be eaten alive by seasoned professionals who know every nook and cranny of the online advertising world. It's not long before your money is spent and you don't have any leads to show for it.

As a rule-of-thumb, I recommend to my clients that they concentrate on all the *free* methods of attracting visitors and generating leads first. I say this because it allows you to determine how best to take full advantage of Web-generated leads before you begin spending money on it to achieve the same result. Perhaps, though, time is of the essence – that is, you have more money than time – so you wish to jump start the process by buying your way to the top of search results in order to engage with Web-generated customers sooner rather than later.

58: Start with a generous budget

Effort: ●●○○○ Cost: $? Reward: ★★★

Having said all I did about being frugal on the Internet, I am now going to tell you, in order to be successful with online advertising, you are probably better off spending your money quickly than spreading your expenditures over a longer period of time. This is because – and this is a theory of mine based on observation, at least – the more often your ad wins a bid for a given set of keywords, the more often it is considered for future bids. And as search words that are of value to you are used in search, you find out quickly whether your product or service – or your ads – are going to work. Once you determine which of your ads are most effective, you can return to optimize them to improve their ROI (Return-on-Investment) over time.

Google AdWords lets you set a maximum price for a Click-Through, but the problem with that is, when ads frequently fail on a bid for keywords their quality score drops. That in turn makes it more expensive for you in the long run to keep your campaign going. It is like saying, *I am going to dive into this pool, but first I will dive into the shallow end to see how I do.* Google AdWords work when you give yourself a generous budget to try it out. The first thing you are trying to determine is what kind of leads you can secure. Later, you can optimize for bidding price, but first, you are trying to determine which keywords will generate leads and which do not.

At the beginning, you want to get visitors, regardless of price. You can optimize later. Paradoxical as it sounds, it can be more expensive in the long run to have a low maximum cost-per-click. So give yourself a handsome budget for about a month, then examine the real data you receive.

59: Measuring the success of ad variations

A slight adjustment to the wording of an advertisement can have a profound impact on its effectiveness. How to know which ads will work best is the subject of many thousands of books and educational materials on the subject, and far beyond the scope of this section, so I will tell you what has worked for me in the past: I experiment with ad variations and use Google AdWords tracking tools to measure their success in my website.

Illustration 23: Google AdWords can be associated with a "success page", defined by a visitor landing on a specified page.

I know what kind of *book titles* work, at least, in the area of semi-technical business books like this one. (1) A solution-oriented title (2) a subtitle with a number in it and (3) the words reflect the contents of the publication.

So much depends on your particular product or service, but one important factor is *how accurately the ad reflects what you are actually offering*, because you pay for each click-through even when the visitor buys nothing or never becomes a lead in your contact management database. You could get many click-through visitors by offering – for example – free music downloads, but if no such thing is on

more money: Google AdWords

your website, it may be a costly exercise in advertising, with no increase in your database of well-targeted leads. Thus, the closer the contents of your web page to the contents of your ad, the higher your visitor-to-lead conversion will be.

60: Home Page as Target Landing Page

Unless your Home Page is specifically designed as a *Target Landing Page*, it is almost always better to use a dedicated Target Landing Page to receive click-through visits from an online ad. (An example of an exception to that rule can be seen on the Netflix Home Page. It is probably because they have a single product – at least, as of typing this).

If a person browsing the Web clicked an ad that offered a *Graphite Reinforced Snowboard*, and landed on your Home Page (or any page on your website not dedicated to the subject of *Graphite Reinforced Snowboard*), the chances they will become a lead or a customer are reduced because the Target Landing Page does not match the search words the visitor began with.

The question to ask yourself is, *does the first page a visitor coming from search sees suggest an answer to the problem they are trying to solve*? For example, if the online ad they clicked said *Bicycle Rental Seattle*, does the *Target Landing Page* they arrive on suggest a solution to the need to rent a bicycle in Seattle?

Today, people are on the hunt for what they want, they know how to search for it, and anything that's not 100% relevant to their search will tend to send them elsewhere.

61: Using an upper limit on spend

Effort: ●●○○○   Cost: $0   Reward: ★★★☆☆

Sheer greed for the top slot in the advertising space sometimes causes companies to get into a bidding war that few can afford. So we need to work out what kind of return-on-investment we can expect for money we spend on such online ads.

Consider this fictitious example: Your company sells replacement windows in the Boston area. The gross profit on each deal is approximately $2,000. In addition, you know that for every one hundred leads you gather, five ultimately become customers. Thus, to break even, a lead may cost no more than $100 (that is, $2,000 x 5%), because it takes twenty of them to make one customer's profit of $2,000. And for every twenty ad-driven visitors to our website, only one surrenders their contact information to become a lead. That means, each click-through from a PPC (Pay-Per-Click) can cost no more than five dollars (one-twentieth of one hundred dollars), just to break even. Clearly, though, we want to make an actual profit, so a break-even scenario is not interesting to us.

The salient factors – or questions – in our calculations are therefore the following:

    A) How profitable is each new customer?

B) What percentage of leads ultimately become customers?

C) What percentage of ad-driven visitors become leads?

D) How much does it cost to generate each Click-Through? (In the numbers we need to reach our sales targets). $3.00.

E) How many new customers do we need to reach our profitability targets?

Our return-on-investment for securing a single customer using online ads = A - (D x 1/B x 1/C)

$2,000 - ($3.00 x 20 x 20) =

$2,000 - $1,200 =

$800

We can see how improvements in any of the factors can have a profound effect on the profitability of our ad campaign. If, for example, by improving our Target Landing Page for a given ad, we doubled the number of its visitors who became leads, we would *halve* the cost of lead generation and increase the resulting customer profitability from $800 to $1,400. That extra profit may allow us to reduce our price slightly – perhaps to become more competitive – or grow our business by increasing our online advertising budget.

No matter how you approach it, knowing the price of a single customer acquisition through online advertising is essential. Google AdWords provides tools to do just that.

62: Using Geographical Filters to reduce costs

Effort: ●●○○○　　Cost: $0　　Reward: ★★★

If you don't support shipping your product outside the country, you don't want people – for example – in Swaziland eating your click-through budget when you know you will never sell to them.

Use the built-in Google AdWords geographical filters to exclude regions where you know you will not do business. Illustration 24 on page 136 is a screen capture from an ad campaign used by a pond accessories company. They targeted regions of the United States during the times of the year when those regions' inhabitants were likely to be involved in maintaining their back-yard ponds. In addition, narrowing the regions where the ads should appear may significantly reduce paying for Click-Throughs that have no chance of ever resulting in business being transacted. This reduces the overall cost of customer acquisition and will almost certainly be part of your AdWords strategy.

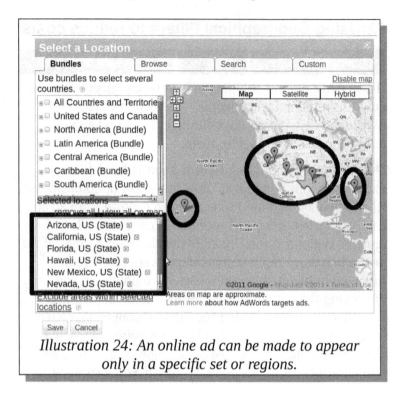

Illustration 24: An online ad can be made to appear only in a specific set or regions.

63: Long Keyword Strategy in online ads

Effort: ●●○○○   Cost: $?   Reward: ★★★☆☆

Just like we outlined in the *Long Keyword Strategy* section beginning on page 28, the same logic applies when creating ads: the more specific your target keywords, the less competition there is for them. Just like with organic search results, it is difficult indeed to get one of your web pages to appear for searches for short, "hot" keywords. If your business is a small, physical jewelry store on Main Street, you will likely not want to bid on the keyword *jewelry*, but will have more success with a keyword that is very specific, such as *tag heuer mens gold automatic 1988*. There will be far fewer searches for that word combination – too few in fact for Google to probably register the count of visits as statistically significant – but the bidding for it will be limited, if there is any, and this will keep your cost per click low and increase the chance that your ad will appear when someone searches using those words.

64: Copying what works

Effort: ●●○○○   Cost: $0   Reward: ★★★☆

Bookshops are crammed with publications on effective advertising, and a complete grounding on how to construct the wording of your online ads is beyond the scope of this one book, so I recommend you look at what already works. Using the keywords you are considering, do a search to see what ads appear. Which of them grab your attention the most?

Most of us have gotten more savvy about what we will – or will not – click online these days, but I still find myself clicking the occasional ad if it really grabs my attention. I tend to click ads that suggest immediate action to solve a problem. For example, *The 5 Ways to Lose Belly Fat Today*. Less compelling for me is a straight sell ad like *Our Free Range Chickens are Tastier than Acme Chickens*. The difference is *active* versus *passive*. Another compelling hook that I like is when the ad contains an uneven number of steps. For example, *17 Ways to Attract Your Perfect Mate,* or *77 Free Ways to Drive Traffic and Generate Leads on your Website.* I don't know why an uneven number is more compelling to me than an even one; perhaps it feels more 'disruptive' than an even number...

65: Making your ads truthful

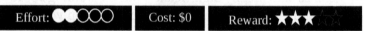

Effort: ●●○○○○   Cost: $0   Reward: ★★★☆☆

Something I learned the hard way in writing books is that the book title and subtitle had better accurately reflect the contents of the book. It is why I put the technical skill required scale on the front cover of this and my previous book. Obvious as it may sound, when a buyer's experience does not match their expectations (e.g., a book's contents do not match the book title and subtitle), they are more likely to put the book back on the shelf or write a more critical review of it.

With Pay-Per-Click advertising, when an ad oversells the product or service, you may indeed increase your Click-Through rate, but far fewer of those visitors will become leads. This can increase your online ad spend significantly. Ideally, *what the ad promises* should match *what the Target Landing Page has to offer.* Keeping your ads truthful increases the percentage of ad-driven visitors that become leads, as outlined in item (C) on page 134, and is a major factor in controlling the costs of your online ad campaign.

66: Economize target URL

Effort: ●●○○○　　Cost: $0　　Reward: ★★★☆☆

The visible destination can be different from the actual destination.

When you construct your Google ad, you can make it display as if the link were to your actual home page, but the actual link is to a specific Target Landing Page. This keeps the ad smaller in appearance and is less likely to distract the potential customer with a long-winded URL.

Illustration 25 on page 140 shows an ad that appears to link directly to the home page of the BBQ Equipment Store's website. In reality, the link is to a Target Landing Page somewhere in their website. (The link also includes information about the ad any Click-Through is coming from, presumably to be used by the website to examine the origins and effectiveness of that particular ad).

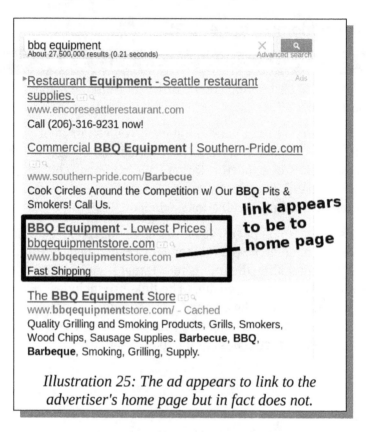

Illustration 25: The ad appears to link to the advertiser's home page but in fact does not.

67: Don't let others harvest your traffic

Google AdWords are displayed in two different contexts on the Web. One is in Google search results, the other is in *contextual advertising space*. You have probably noticed by now how Google ads enrich your Web browsing experience no matter where you go on the Internet.

Page 140

You are probably used to seeing ads for things that are of interest to you, but on websites which, you would think, couldn't possibly know what your interests are. Let's say your hobby was collecting model trains. You are browsing your local city's online newspaper, and you wonder how on Earth ads relating to model trains appear in the ads section of the newspaper website! How did they know you were interested in model trains? Firstly, the newspaper website itself knows nothing about you. They do, however, have a code snippet on their website that Google controls, and Google *does* know a lot about you. If you use Gmail they know from the contents of your emails what kind of subjects you are interested in. They also know what kind of searches you have performed, even if you were not logged into Google when you performed any of those searches, because they can infer a lot about who a person is by their location on the Internet and cookies in their browser, left behind from previous searches. And lastly, they know that your physical computer has performed such-and-such searches in the past. All that is, of course, roughly speaking. I don't know for sure which exact combination of mechanisms they use to get those perfectly targeted ads in your face as you wander the Internet, but the important thing to know here is, search engines know enough about you to place ads in front of you that maximize the possibility of Click-Throughs.

Using a Google service called AdSense, businesses can make money by placing Google contextual ads on their websites. When visitors click such an ad, a portion of the ad revenue goes to the owner of the website that displayed the ad. It is a way to "cash in" on the value of the website traffic a website has generated.

When you bid for ad placements, you can specify if you would like your ads to appear – in addition to search results in general – within the gargantuan network of Google AdSense ads and in front of people who are simply surfing the Web and who Google knows are interested in your kind of product or service.

You can also target specific websites. For example, you can specify that you want a particular ad to appear in the Google AdSense on the *American Association for Retired Persons*' website (www.aarp.com), or on a list of websites. What you definitely do *not* want, is for a competitor of yours to place *their* ads on *your* website; not after all the hard work you've done and money you've spent attracting your own website visitors in the first place.

If you use Google AdSense to generate ad revenue from traffic on *your* website, remember that your competitors may be able to place ads for *their* products or services right on your website, assuming they support AdSense on their website. A travesty, or course, because it is a way for your competitors to target your potential shoppers directly. It would be like Macy's of New York displaying their ads in the aisles of Bloomingdales. The only way of stopping your competitors from doing it to you, is to not use Google AdSense on your website.

68: Don't use your own company name

When constructing your Google ad, it is usually best to avoid the use of your company name in the ad directly. There are some exceptions to this rule, but for small companies with no brand recognition on the Web, the precious real estate within the tiny Google ad is too early to introduce your company brand to potential customers. Once they have become a lead, however, it is time to begin the process of building your brand in their mind.

Illustration 26 on page 144 shows a partial screen capture of the Google ads that appeared when I searched for *bbq supplies*. You can see how the ads focus on a *solution* that the company has to offer. The objective of the ad is to entice the viewer to click the ad, of course, and visit the website. Once you have brought that visitor to your website – whether it is with an ad or from organic search results – the next stage of the dance begins. That is, the Engage stage, as outlined in the Introduction on page 21. It is in the *Engage* stage that you introduce your brand to the potential customer.

Illustration 26: The only clue to the company name in a well constructed Google ad is in the link URL.

69: Exclude same-word, unrelated areas

Keywords can have different meanings in different markets. In English, if my business rents tuxedos, a *tie* has a very specific meaning. I do not want to pay for click-throughs from people who are look for railroad ties.

Google AdWords allow you to opt out of bidding for keyword combinations if certain words also appear in the context. Using the example of the tie in the previous paragraph, I would set up my ad to bid for *tie* in the context of *tuxedo rental*, but not if the word *railroad* also appears in that same context. This reduces the number of people who are absolutely not in my target market who might otherwise click my ad without ever having a chance of becoming a customer. Illustration 27, below, shows how you can avoid displaying your ad for tuxedo rental when a person is searching for railroad ties. Note the minus sign before the keywords "railroad tie". You can use this feature when you are adding keywords to a Google Ad Group.

Enter one keyword per line. Add keywords by spreadsheet

```
"tuxedo rental"
"shirt and tie rental"
renting a tuxedo in bellevue
-"railroad tie"
```

Illustration 27: The search words "railroad tie" are excluded from the keywords to avoid displaying the ad to those searching with the word "tie" in the context of railroad ties.

70: Paying for what you can get for free

Effort: ●●○○○○   Cost: $0   Reward: ★★★☆☆

Have you ever seen a company appear in the ads section of search results and also in the organic section right below it? They might pay two dollars for you to click their ad, but get your patronage for free if you click their entry in organic search results.

Be aware of those ads you might be paying for when you could be receiving the same traffic for free through organic search results. Personally, I like to click *organic search results* more than ads. I feel that there is usually a real reason for an organization appearing in organic search results over those that paid to be there. There are also unproven suggestions that search engines give preference in organic search results to those websites that are also spending money on related online ads with the same search engine. I, personally, have not seen specific evidence to prove that, but you never know...

Communications

The term *Social Media* describes some of the tools used in the grand effort to connect with future and existing customers. *Communications,* on the other hand, speaks to *why* we are doing all of this work. It is also action oriented. *Social Media* is about tools; *Communications* is about action. And action is what is needed.

Imagine for a moment that you own a physical shoe store; visitors enter your store, look around briefly then walk out without sharing a single word with you or any of your employees. For every two hundred visitors, you sell a single pair of shoes. All that rent, experience, bills and life energy invested into the business and at the last moment, you do a Mr. Freeze with every potential customer. That is, you ignore them.

Compare that to the results if, with every walk-in, you were to strike up a conversation. It sounds corny, but asking a walk-in possible customer *can I help you find the right pair of shoes, sir/ma'am*? increases the probability of a sale. The moment your potential customer opens their mouth to respond, a relationship has started, however small it might be to begin with. Even when a sale does not occur, the prospect has invested something in the relationship, and the business operator learns something about their own market and product. With each new conversation, the business operator gets more engaged, knowledgeable and capable. Walmart, famous for cutting costs to the bone, still sees the value in paying an employee to stand inside the front door, making contact with as many arriving shoppers as possible. The position of *Greeter* has been added to the Walmart's lore of cost-effective ways to engage with their target market. And it is not just Walmart that does it. How many times have you heard the phrase *Can I help you find something* or, on the way out the door or at the cashier, *Did you find everything you were looking for?*

Some of it is simply about being polite. Companies want people to believe they at least care enough to ask, but the real reason is, making direct contact increases the brand value in the mind of the potential customer and increases sales in the long run.

It is just like that on the Web. The daily or hourly grind of making direct contact with members of your target market – with the same message no matter what channel you use to develop that contact – is at the core of success using all these trendy tools (Facebook, Twitter, etc.).

Success begets success

And just like in the submarine story on page 12, there is an inflection point (or *Tipping Point,* to use the name of the book written by Malcolm Gladwell) where the return on investment begins to feed on itself. One of the significant factors to keeping a page on a website appearing at the top of search results is for it to get clicked in search results. The very act of a search results item being clicked increases the chances that Google will display it higher up in search results next time! So *staying there* is easier than *getting there*.

71:Using the 1-1-1 formula

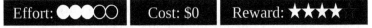

Every day, make 1 blog posting, 1 Facebook update and 1 Tweet.

You can certainly overdo Facebook postings. Personally, I use Facebook for a mix of both business and friendships, and when I see too many postings coming in from a single contact, I block that person's posts from appearing altogether. I don't want to hear from any one person that often, and I suspect many people do the same when they get inundated. So, keep Facebook to a maximum of two postings a day. Better, though, to keep it to one.

Twitter is a bit more forgiving. Tweets are short and limited.

72: Open your Facebook comments to your contacts

Effort: ●○○○○	Cost: $0	Reward: ★★★★★

You have a Facebook account for your business. Instead of commenting on and liking images and other objects on others' Facebook accounts, *share* them on your own. For example, suppose your business were a lighting fixtures company, and one of your suppliers announced a new line of floor lamps. What many such businesses do is click the *Like* button and/or comment on the image or announcement that the supplier posted. Rather than doing that, if you share the album or announcement on your Facebook account, *your* Facebook friends can comment on your posting and thus, contribute to *your* FB content.

I often feel the desire to add comments or click the *Like* button on one of my FB friends' contributions only to see that the posting is *outside* my friend's account, so I can do neither. The opportunity to contribute content to my friend's FB account is therefore lost.

> If you see a Facebook page, posting, image or album that you feel could add real value to your account – and maybe spark a conversation – use the Facebook *Share* feature (instead of *Like* or *Comment*) to expose the object to your Facebook friends. This allows your friends to increase the content value of your Facebook account.

73: The same message repeated everywhere

Effort: ●●●●○   Cost: $0   Reward: ★★★★☆

It's tempting to believe you can find customers by living in Twitter or by concentrating on Facebook alone – and there may be some businesses out there that survive totally on one of these community websites – but the Web success stories I have witnessed have worked all channels simultaneously and with the same message.

Community websites like Facebook and Twitter (there are *many* others) are like magnets to those of us with a touch of ADD (Attention Deficit Disorder). It is easy to get pulled in many different directions, and end up covering a new topic with every new conversation. That's fine if your Facebook account is for recreation, but if it is there to support your business, you need to stick to your subject – and to your message – every time. Let's look at an example:

Your company manufactures and sells organic, 100% green, laundry and other detergent products. A competitive strength is that your products are priced – per wash – at the same level as traditional detergents. Your subject is *detergents* and your message is *organic, green* and *price competitive*. Press releases, website home page, blog postings, Tweets and Facebook postings should all be delivering the same message over and over. When someone – for example – makes a Facebook comment on your account that distracts from your message, consider deleting it or at least ignoring it.

Creating your Web success is more of an exercise in orchestration than a solo performance. Consistent messaging through all channels is what builds brand and ultimately leads to customers and revenue.

Converting visitors into leads

SEO (Search Engine Optimization) generates traffic on your website, but what happens next? Website traffic on its own is worth little unless you can turn some of it into sales leads – the contact details of potential customers – that form the basis of future sales.

If there is a purpose for a Marketing Department, it is to supply the Sales Department with a constant flow of new potential customers. For small companies, their website is a central tool of the

Marketing Department, and we know it has done its job when sales leads are flowing from it.

In this chapter, we talk about harvesting all that traffic we hope to generate, by turning it into quality, usable sales leads. That means, primarily, gathering the contact details of website visitors, along with other facts such as their purchasing time frame, potential sales volume, and other demographics that may help us during the sales process.

The better we implement the following recommendations, the higher our website sales leads Capture Rate is going to be. In other words, for every thousand visitors to our website, how many of them will become sales leads? Revenue volume will track Capture Rate. If we double the Capture Rate, we may double the sales volume, so this step is every bit as important as generating traffic.

74: Mobile CSS: Making your website usable on hand-held devices

Mobile CSS is a way to make your website appear differently when it is being viewed on a mobile device (iPhone, Blackberry, etc.). This is essential if your visitors are likely to be accessing your website using a smart phone or other hand-held device with a reduced screen size. The competitive opportunity here is enormous because – as of late 2011 – the vast majority of websites do not directly support hand-held visitors, including your competitors most likely. It is probably because use of hand-held devices increased so rapidly over the past several years, most organizations are still playing catch-up.

Without building a totally new website, the browser can be instructed to use a different Style Sheet (CSS) to display the website if it is being viewed using a mobile device. Because the website's Style Sheet controls its appearance – including the size of images, text and the web page itself – an alternate Style Sheet for hand-held devices allows us to make a "smaller website". We can also remove parts of the page that are not essential, for example, additional navigation options in the page footer, and so on.

The location of a typical alternate Style Sheet for hand-held devices looks like this:

```
http://www.myfancywebsite.com/mobile.css
```

In addition to creating your alternate Style Sheet, a small change is made to each page on your website to "tell the browser" to use the alternate Style Sheet if the visitor is using a mobile device.

The quickest way to add support for a mobile device is to take a copy of the current Style Sheet (e.g. *mystyles.css*) that controls how your website appears currently, rename it (for example, to *mobile.css*) and place it in the same directory as your current Style Sheet. Then, add a line to every page of your website to refer to it:

```
<link rel="stylesheet"
href="http://www.myfancywebsite.com/mobile.css"
type="text/css" media="handheld" />
```

Support for mobile CSS is not a trivial task, but it can usually be done in a couple of days. Using CSS instead of building a new website, means that you continue to use the same content, but it simply appears differently on hand-held devices.

About half of all website visitor traffic today – taken as an aggregate of all traffic – is made using a hand-held device. It may be significantly different in your organization's case. Some companies sell to the "soccer mom" market, while others sell to government agencies, so your market type, among other factors, will determine what percentage of visitors are likely to be using hand-held devices.

75: Supporting Apple Add-to-Favorites

Effort: ●●○○○	$0	Reward: ★★☆☆☆

The following code allows visitors using Apple products (Apple Mac, iPad, etc.) to add a web page to their Favorites with a single click.

```
<link rel="apple-touch-icon" href="/filename.png" />
```

The image is a 57x57 pixel icon that is stored on your website.

76: Controlling shrink/grow of web page with the Viewport tag

Effort: ●●○○○	$0	Reward: ★★☆☆☆

You have likely seen by now how websites viewed on many Apple and other products can be "shrunk" or "grown" by a "pinch" or "expand" finger gesture on the touch-sensitive screen of the device. Depending on how your website needs to behave on such devices, you may need to allow or restrict that shrink/grow functionality.

Use a Viewport tag to control if mobile visitors can shrink/grow the website. It will look something like the following code example, which I found on the web. It sets the page to fit to the width of the mobile device, and says it cannot be shrunk or grown:

```
<meta name="viewport" content="width=device-width,initial-scale=1,user-scalable=no" />
```

77: Point backlinks to Target Landing Pages

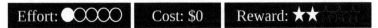

Effort: ●○○○○   Cost: $0   Reward: ★★☆☆☆

I often see a very well written article on a public forum that links back to the contributor's home page or other page not focused on converting that visitor to a lead.

Let's recap what the primary purpose of a website is for the vast majority of small businesses: *it is to generate leads*. You know you have successfully generated a lead when you have gathered the visitor's contact information. It is what defines the point at which a visitor becomes a lead.

When you make a posting to a forum, blog or other such website, with a view to creating a link back to *your* website, what happens when someone actually clicks that link and visits your website for the first time? Do they simply arrive at your home page? Well, you can do a lot more to draw them closer to becoming a lead, and that is, to provide a link on that original posting to a page on your website dedicated to converting that visitor to a lead. Such a page is called a Target Landing Page, and the only real purpose of a Target Landing Page is to secure the contact information of the visitor.

> When you add a backlink to your off-page blog posting, point that link to a dedicated Target Landing Page. For example, if I were an accountant writing an article on Bank of America's Small Business Forum about filling out ones tax returns, I might add a link – titled "More on this subject" – at the bottom of the article, pointing to a page on my website that offers "The 7 Easiest Ways to Maximize Your Tax Rebate". On that page, I ask for the visitor's contact information before giving them the free PDF.

78: Effective Target Landing Pages

| Effort: ●●●○○ | Cost: $0 | Reward: ★★★★ |

On the journey to converting a visitor to a customer, the visitor must first become a *lead*. The progression is from *Stranger* to *Visitor* to *Lead* to *Customer*. There are many sub-steps in that journey, of course, and there is a deep and broad science behind sales funnel management, but the only part of this journey a Target Landing Page (TLP) has to worry about is converting a *Visitor* into a *Lead*.

This is what an effective TLP looks like: Very roughly speaking, about one-third of it is a *visualization of a solution or satisfied customer*, and the rest is an *Invitation to Engage*. That is, in the case of a TLP that is entirely visible above the fold. (The fold is the lowest part of a web page you can see without having to scroll down). The Netflix example in Illustration 29 on page 161 is a TLP that is contained entirely above the fold. Some TLPs are much longer, sometimes containing a lot more information – from testimonials to videos to success stories – but for our purposes here, we will focus on the above-the-fold kind.

A visualization of a satisfied customer is usually a picture where a visitor to your site can see the solution or "see themselves" as they might appear if they buy your product or service. For example, Netflix's TLP shows a happy family sitting together watching a movie about to start on their TV, as highlighted in Illustration 29 on page 161. Excluding the standard footer links at the bottom of the page, the rest of the page is covered in various ways for the visitor to sign up as a lead. That *Invitation to Engage* is heavily reinforced by Netflix's offer of one month's free movie rentals.

Image of happy customer

Invitation to Engage

Illustration 28: A good Target Landing Page contains an image of a happy customer and an Invitation to Engage

Look at the live example www.bike-repair-seattle.com to see a very typical appearance of a *Target Landing Page*.

Illustration 29 on page 161 shows the relative screen real estate used by the *image of a happy customer* and the *Invitation to Engage*. You may have only one TLP on your website – and it may be your actual Home Page – but it should be constructed in a manner similar to that in Illustration 29.

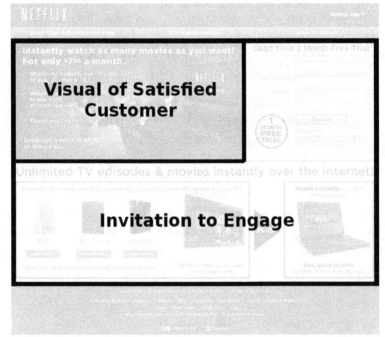

Illustration 29: Netflix's home page - a Target Landing Page that many people are familiar with.

79: Add a contact information capture form

Effort: ●●●○○	Cost: $10	Reward: ★★★☆☆

Years ago, it was enough to offer a toll-free number on your website, and perhaps a basic email-us link, as a way for visitors to contact the website owners. As part of the critical *Engage* stage in growing your business on the Web, you will benefit from a more structured way of gathering visitor contact information, especially if the numbers grow quickly. You might also need, depending on your type of business, a way to manage email communications with your growing list of leads.

If you only need to manage a relatively small number of leads, consider a program like EmailMeForm (www.emailmeform.com). It allows you to specify the types of information you would like to gather (e.g. Name, Address, email address, phone number, etc.) and it automatically builds the HMTL code for you. You then simply paste it into your web page and voilà, your website can accept contact information from visitors. Some great features of such a service are that it (a) builds the code for you, (b) manages the redirection of the visitor after they enter their info, (c) allows you to specify recipients, (d) allows encryption if needed, and offers many other features.

If you need to follow up with your gathered leads in a more structured and scalable way, you will need a contact management system (CMS) like allclients.com, aweber.com, icontact.com or constantcontact.com. There are many others out there, but these four are some of the more popular. As well as storing the leads in a flexible database, these systems allow you to communicate *en masse* with large numbers of your contacts. They deal with spam issues, opt-ins, opt-outs, email formatting and a variety of marketing programs. You may not have even noticed it, but likely you have received many emails via these contact management systems already.

> At the time of writing this, www.icontact.com was offering a 100% free service to those who have a limited number of contacts. Start there and examine how you can use this feature to manage the leads you generate. If the numbers begin to grow, having everything in such a database will make it much easier to manage and maximize the conversion rate of leads to customers when you reach that point.

80: Offer something of value for contact information

Effort: ●●●○○   Cost: $?   Reward: ★★★☆☆

The contact information of a visitor to your website, especially if they are in the market for what you sell, is valuable. When they willingly give to you their contact information, they have *de facto* become a lead, and leads are worth money.

In this new age of *Inbound Marketing*, it is the *future customer* who will decide whether they want to hear from you. In the old days of *Outbound Marketing*, you might have bought the contact information of thousands of individuals – turning them into unsuspecting sales leads – then marketed aggressively to each and every one of them in the hopes that a few customers would shake out of the process. Today, you have to offer something of real value before they offer you their contact information.

It might be a brochure, a trial size product, or a free foot massage for new clients. Remember that it is *not an incentive to purchase* – like a discount coupon would be – but it is a*n incentive to begin a relationship*. That is an important difference because the purpose of your *Target Landing Page* is to turn a visitor into a *lead*, not a customer. That comes later. Many website owners miss this subtlety; they try to skip directly to the *Close* stage, skipping the *Engage* stage. For small companies – that is, companies whose website visitors are seeing for the first time – the purpose is to begin that relationship that some day, may result in a sale.

81: Effective Secondary Target Landing Pages

Effort: ●●●○○	$0	Reward: ★★★

A *Secondary* Target Landing Page (STLP) has an additional purpose: it provides valuable information to its visitors, and a section of the page is dedicated to doing just that.

A reasonable rule-of-thumb is to devote the bottom third of the visible part of the page to the information that attracted the visitor to the page, with the top two-thirds performing the function of a regular Target Landing Page. If the average computer screen is a thousand or so pixels tall, then the top 700 pixels might be devoted to a *visual of a satisfied customer* plus an *Invitation to Engage*.

One of the central purposes of your daily blogging is to create lots of potential search matches for people searching for what you offer. A well-constructed blog entry has the intended keywords in the right place and a valuable piece of information on the page itself, which all together is what attracted the visitor in the first place. It goes like this: someone on the Internet is looking for information on how competitive bicycles are constructed. They Google *diy competitive bicycle construction*, and are presented with a page from the website www.kirklandcycle.com that talks about that exact topic in the bottom one-third of the web page. The top two-thirds of the page contain the *visual of a satisfied customer* plus an *Invitation to Engage*. The visual is an image of someone putting the finishing touches to a classy looking bike and the Invitation to Engage is an offer of a free monthly bicycle owner's newsletter.

I made most of that up of course, but the mechanics of how a Secondary Target Landing Page are about that simple and don't vary much. Some pages show the happy customers on the right hand side, or in a variety of images, or in one of many other formats. I like the "Netflix model" because it is crisp and clean and I will wager that their marketing team put a lot of resources into it.

```
┌─────────────────────────────────────────┐
│  ┌──────────────────────────┐           │
│  │                          │           │
│  │  Visual of satisfied     │           │
│  │  customer                │           │
│  │                          │           │
│  └──────────────────────────┘           │
│                                          │
│         Invitation to Engage             │
│                                          │
│  ┌─────────────────────────────────────┐ │
│  │                                     │ │
│  │      Valuable Information            │ │
│  │                                     │ │
│  └─────────────────────────────────────┘ │
└─────────────────────────────────────────┘
```

Illustration 30: a Secondary Target Landing aims to attract visitors from Organic Search Results

82: Each STLP speaks to one customer type

Effort: ●●●○○   Cost: $0   Reward: ★★★

A customer type is defined by a single customer problem you solve and a Secondary Target Landing Page is focused on that one customer problem, even though you might solve several problems for the one physical customer.

For example, a company sells the following three types of liquid nutrition supplements *Glucosamine, Multi-vitamin* and a *Digestive Aid* as three distinct products, each sold separately and each targeted at solving a specific problem for a customer.

Even though one customer may buy several unrelated products from you, when a potential customer searches the Web, they always do so with a *single problem* in mind. For example, a person searches for *liquid vitamin supplement* and follows the suggestions offered by the search engine. They are unlikely to search for *liquid vitamin supplement joint problems* because people don't search for solutions to two problems with the one search. Because a potential customer searches for a solution to *a single problem at a time*, we tailor a Secondary Target Landing Page (and sometimes a regular Target Landing Page) to focus on *one problem alone*, or to be more specific, our specific product that solves that single problem.

In the case of the liquid supplements company example, each blog entry – with respect to its function as a STLP – will speak to one of the products.

Do you sell more than one product? Do you solve more than one customer problem? Let's imagine you have 30 SKUs (Stock Keeping Units) – like the variety of sizes of the basic three liquid supplement products I mentioned a few paragraphs ago. If you were to place one of each SKU on a table, could you group them together with respect to what problem each solves? If you were the liquid supplements company, you should have three groups of products on the table. For the purposes of generating leads on the Web, a Secondary Target Landing Page will concern itself with the product in *only one* of those groups.

The liquid supplements company example is a simple one, so let's look at an example of a business where the "problem a product solves" is a little murky. Imagine you have a jewelry business. You sell new and pre-owned watches, rings, pendants, bracelets and necklaces. How do you group your products into groups that "solve a specific problem"?

Price is probably the most significant defining characteristic of how products may be grouped by the problems they solve. Of course, a one thousand dollar diamond ring does not solve the same problem as a one thousand dollar Seiko watch. So, we group products by type, then by price. You can see this in effect on websites, where products are grouped by price ranges; you select the price range to narrow down the list of products to be displayed.

Likely you can group your customer type by price range. Still, a given individual may consider $200 to be too high a price for a watch, but feel that $4,000 is too little to spend on a diamond engagement ring. So we consider that one physical person to be two different customers – that is, from the point of gathering leads – so we group by product type first, then price range. And for each result, we use a specific *Secondary Target Landing Page* to address its respective problem. The problem *I need a silver necklace for about $1,000* might have its own STLP.

You probably don't want to create on your website an STLP for every possible combination of product and price range, but I have found that many companies already have their website categorized in a way that supports this. They already have natural groupings on the website that provide pages we can turn into STLPs.

> List the problems your products or services solve. For example: a homeopathic products company sells a dozen or so remedies in pill form. The problems they solve are: (1) Air sickness, (2) Indigestion, (3) Afternoon fatigue and (4) Jet lag. Do you have a specific STLP on your website – for each problem you solve – that allows a visitor to engage with you and become a lead?

83: Consistent menu bar throughout website

Effort: ●●●○○ Cost: $0 Reward: ★★★☆☆

I remember visiting Niagara Falls at a time when there was so much mist thrown up by the raging river and low cloud cover, I could see as far as my clenched fist. Clenched, because it was tightly gripping the guide rail as I inched my way along the viewing trail. The lack of visibility would have been completely disorienting were it not for the hand rail, which was at the same height and position relative to the trail every step of the way.

When someone visits your website for the first time, you want them to become a lead as soon as possible, but they may – more likely than not – wish to take a stroll around your website first. Before they agree to enter their precious contact information in the hopes of getting your wonderful newsletter or free product sample, a visitor may check you out by looking at your *About Us* section, the *Clients* or *Testimonials* section, or they may even just examine your website for a sense of quality and professionalism.

One significant quality aspect of a website is the consistency (or lack thereof) of the main navigation bar. The more inconsistent that menu bar is – as a visitor browses various pages on your website – the less likely they are to offer up their contact details to become a lead.

Keep the navigation bar constant throughout the website. It will increase the percentage of visitors that become leads.

For example: suppose your main navigation bar has the following items: *Home / Products / Clients / Support / About us / Contact us*. A visitor clicks *Products* to visit your products page but now, the menu bar changes to a list of product groups. The visitor has to reorient themselves to the new navigation structure, increasing the chance that they will leave your website.

84: Using an industrial-strength tool to build your website

Effort: ●●●●○   Cost: $400   Reward: ★★★★★

A Web Content Management System (WCM) is a program that runs on the server that hosts your website, and allows you to manage the content of your website through a browser. They are – in the business of building websites – the best thing since sliced bread.

I still hear about companies that continue to use their own, home-grown Web Content Management System internally. WCMs have gotten so sophisticated – some dedicated WCM manufacturers have dozens if not hundreds of developers working tirelessly on their product – it is hard to imagine a company would want the expense of building their own. Companies offer many excuses for sticking with their home-grown system – from "we have special requirements" to "we don't need all that fancy functionality" - but ninety-nine times out of a hundred, it is both a waste of money and a squandering of opportunity.

Why does it happen? Why does a company insist on building their own tools for building and managing their website? This is why: a developer or development team in the company is tasked with managing, replacing or growing their company's website. This team doesn't have any experience of WCMs, and their website has hitherto been maintained using a HTML Editor (like FrontPage, Home Site, Dreamweaver, etc.) so they satisfy a couple of requirements by writing a script or two. Before long, they are expanding the script into a home-grown little machine for spitting out web pages. Before you know it, the company's website is totally dependent on the new tool and it becomes progressively more costly to ween the organization off the darn thing. Development team members now also have a vested interest in keeping the tool alive – job security comes to mind – and good money is thrown after bad until everyone eventually wakes up.

> Expertise is owned by individuals; process is owned by a corporation.

Dependency on individual developers is bad for business because, sooner or later, developers move on. The money spent on adding new features – features that are already available, tried and tested in the marketplace – eats into profits. The missed opportunities of powerful features you never even heard of, is also bad for business.

You need an industrial strength WCM to create, grow and maintain your website. Bite the bullet and make a plan today for getting rid of your home-grown and move to a Commercial-Off-The-Shelf (COTS) system. Examples are WordPress, Drupal, Joomla, Magento, ExpressionEngine and Big Medium.

85: Qualifying leads to optimize sales

Effort: ●●●○○	Cost: $0	Reward: ★★★☆

Too early or too late.

There is nothing more frustrating for sales folks than to receive leads that are not properly qualified. What does that mean? The sales person makes a call to a lead only to discover that the person at the other end of the phone is not in the actual market to buy, or the timing is not right.

On the other end of the scale, many ready-to-buy prospects wither on the vine for want of a simple sales call. According to Marketing Sherpa, *70-90% of leads provided by Marketing to Sales are never followed up on.* My own feeling about that is, much of the problem is caused by sales people losing confidence in the company's official lead generation process, and they focus on other ways to secure customers.

You've probably noticed once or twice during your own personal experiences on the Web, an online submittal form asks you if you are considering a purchase, for example, (a) *immediately,* (b) w*ithin three months,* (c) *3-6 months,* etc..

This information is invaluable for sales people – or marketing people, if more lead management is required before Sales takes over – in improving the efficiency of the sales process by only spending time on leads that might turn into customers.

For every hour a sales person spends pursuing leads, the more they know about the lead in advance, the more money they will make for the company and for themselves. In addition, their confidence in their marketing department's lead generation process will inspire them to pursue more leads. Another – perhaps more cynical – way to look at it is, it's the Marketing Department's job to remove the Sales Department's every last excuse for not closing sales. And the "lousy lead" excuse is one of the most common.

Real potential customers don't mind answering a few questions. When a person has a problem to solve, and they think they may have found a website with a likely solution, they will answer a few basic questions, so don't be afraid to ask. When a person is not really in the market, but is just browsing, a few questions online is usually enough to send them away so they stop wasting your time. Such pseudo-prospects drain the resources of a sales team, so it's good to get them off the list early.

Let's look at an example from a customer's point of view:

Imagine you are a house owner. It's September and you need a local company to replace the windows in your house before winter arrives. You know it's probably going to be in the $20,000 price range, and you've found a website of a windows replacement company in your city. You are on the company's *Contact Us* page. It is asking for your contact information (e.g. name, phone number) , but also, asks you for three more pieces of information. You are asked for your *ZIP code*, the *square footage of your house* and *when you plan to get the job done*. From the ZIP code, they can tell what level of quality / fit-and-finish you will pay for; if you live in Beverly Hills, the sales person won't offer to install plastic window frames. The square footage will tell them how many windows are likely to be in the house, and when you plan to get the job done will help them decide when to call you. All that information can dramatically increase the close percentage – or the "batting average" as they say in baseball circles – of a sales person.

When you are gathering leads from your website, be sure to ask questions that will help your sales people decide what to do with each lead. Leads can be delivered to Sales close to the time frame of when they said they are likely to make a purchase.

All this sounds like I am talking about a large company that has a "Sales Department" and a "Marketing Department". Your company might be you, your spouse and two employees. Perhaps one person does all the marketing and another does the sales. Whatever your organization's size or structure, qualifying leads saves time and money.

86: Defining the ideal lead

Effort: ●●●○○ | Cost: $0 | Reward: ★★★☆☆

This action item feeds into the previous action item. How do you determine the criteria for qualification, which tells you the quality of the leads you are gathering?

In every corporation I've ever worked for – including the company Bocada which I co-founded – there was always a misalignment with what Sales expected and what Marketing delivered. It seemed the hardest thing in the world to get to the point where Marketing understood and agreed to deliver what Sales needed. That might be a typical problem in an established corporation, but it's not a whole lot different in a two- or six-person organization. *What does the ideal sales lead look like?*

It's actually not that hard to work out. Anyone who has had to sell whatever your company has to offer, can usually tell you – with a little coaching – what the ideal sales lead looks like.

If we were to look at the tiny fictitious company *The Seattle Bicycle Repair Company,* it would be easy: the ideal lead *has a broken bicycle, wants it fixed now, lives within ten miles of the shop, and can spend fifty dollars.* In my Bocada company – years ago, anyway – the ideal lead *(1) had tried to solve the problem internally, (2) backs up data every night on hundreds of computers, (3) has more than one backup product, and (4) has the money today to spend $100 per computer to solve the problem.* Our Bocada sales team knew from experience that prospects who had tried – and failed – to solve the problem internally were far more likely to buy than those who did not. Then it was usually just a question of finding out whether they had the budget or not. Still, knowing those four answers was a far more reliable predictor than any wish they expressed to us or admiration they voiced for our product.

Defining what the ideal lead looks like, helps us filter out – or postpone – visitors to our website who do not meet our criteria significantly and who are likely therefore to waste our time. Whatever those criteria are can be turned into form questions on a page of your website. The only hard part is to determine what those questions are. Remember, any visitor who has a problem to solve – assuming your website looks like it might solve it – will be more willing to offer up their contact information and answer a few questions. Illustration 31 displays a form designed to learn whether an interested candidate has ever had a reflexology session before; the organization knows from experience that such inquirers are 80% likely to sign up, compared to 20% if they have never had a reflexology session before. This information might be enough to determine whether or not to give the prospect a return call.

Your business likely has such criteria too.

If your company sells high end lighting fixtures, a key question might be whether the inquirer is a *consumer* or a *designer*. If you are an online jewelry store, a key question might be the visitor's age group.

In my Siteleads.net business, the qualifying questions are (1) *Have you been in business for three or more years*, (2) *Have you sold your product or service a number of times already* and (3) *do you have the resources to nurture a Web presence for the long term*?

Web Traffic Magnet 2

Service inquiry
Please answer the questions below and press

Email	
Phone Number	☐ - ☐ - ☐ ### ### ####
Website	http://
Timeframe to buy:	○ Immediately ○ Within 3 months ○ Later
Reflexology before?	☐ I have done Reflexology before

Image Verification

P N V S Please enter the text from the image:
[_____] [Refresh Image] [What's This?]

Submit

Illustration 31: A typical contact information form embedded in a web page

---

This process of getting the lead characteristics into such sharp focus may result in fewer leads being handed to Sales, but those you do deliver are far superior income generating opportunities.

87: Using RSS Feeds to bring visitors back

Effort: ●●●○○   Cost: $0   Reward: ★★★

An RSS Feed is a feature you can add to your website that allows visitors to add your website or page to a "Reader" that will tell them when the website or page changes. It means the visitor does not have to return every day to see if there is something new, but rather, wait until their Reader Service tells them something has changed.

A visitor might be very happy that they found your website but may – in this world of a million distractions – forget about it a day later, even though your website had something very valuable to offer.

RSS Feed support on your website means the visitor doesn't have to take the bigger step of giving you their full contact information – which they may not be prepared to do yet – so this feature serves as a half-way-house of sorts towards the visitor becoming a lead.

> To see a list of news feeds widgets you can add to your website, Google *rss news feed widget*. Depending on the one you select, it will likely provide all the HTML you need to paste into your own website. Illustration 32 shows how the feature appears on a typical website.

For those who use a Web Content Management System (WCM), the feature is built right into the program already, and is often included in default templates that come with the product. Once it is installed in your website, visitors who are familiar with this Internet feature may use it to flag part or all of your website for later notification should anything be added or changed on your site.

*Illustration 32: An RSS Feeds feature that has been
added to a website as it typically appears*

88: Knowing the source of your leads

Effort: ●○○○○　　Cost: $0　　Reward: ★★★

Knowing the source of each lead tells you how much they
cost. If you spend $2,000 a month on Internet ads, and that
turns into one hundred usable leads, you know that each of
them costs twenty dollars. If *organic search results* deliver
another eighty such leads, you can measure that against
your efforts in *search engine optimization.*

How do you know how many leads were generated from
each source? Answer: Dedicated, unpublished pages.

When you buy online ads, each should be sent to its own,
dedicated Targeted Landing Page (TPL). What's more, that
page should not be linked to from anywhere else on the
website or the Web in general. Only the specific ad you are
paying for links to that page. Any seasoned advertising

executive will tell you that even a slight change in the wording of an ad can have a profound effect on its efficacy. As you experiment with different variations of a given ad on the Internet, each with its own dedicated TPL, you can measure (1) how many visitors are sent to the TPL and (2) how many of those ultimately become leads.

Each of your TPLs should have a marker of some kind so that when you examine the aggregated data – from all the ads you placed – in your contact database, you know which leads came from which ad.

For example: you have three distinct ads sending visitors to three distinct TPLs. Each TPL has a pre-populated, hidden field – let's call it *Source* – that arrives in the contact database along with the information entered by the prospect. The input form on the first ad is coded with "Ad1" in the hidden Source field. You can see in Table 1 on page 181 how five of the leads in the contact database are marked with the ad that they originated from.

Secondary Target Landing Pages (STLP), described on page 164, may each have their own dedicated *Source* marker, but it will be more efficient to group many or all of them together. For example, all blog posting pages (which are STLPs) will have the same *Source* marker because we can use Google Analytics to see which blog pages get the most traffic and measure those results against the number of leads that came from blog pages, as illustrated in the two last rows of Table 1 on page 181.

Name	Email	Age	Source
John	john@gmail.com	45	Ad1
Mary	mary@abc1com	34	Ad1
Joe	joe@ibm.com	41	Ad1
Bob	bob@microsoft.com	22	Ad2
Jane	Jane.smith@eds.com	28	Ad3
Tim	tim-t@company.com	43	Blog
Johnny	jhny@myplace.com	33	Blog

Table 1 The source of each lead is sent by the input form on its dedicated, hidden Target Landing Page. In this example, five leads were generated from the three ads: Ad1, Ad2, Ad3.

You can see it takes a bit of legwork to know where your leads are coming from, but the cost of *not* knowing is tremendous. Perhaps two of the twelve ads are sending the majority of quality leads, or organic search is delivering most of the leads at a fraction of the cost of paid advertising. Knowing where leads originate may save you a lot of money or, better still, may allow you to pour a bigger investment into those parts of your marketing plan that are delivering the best results.

89: Knowing which equipment visitors are using

Some time in the spring of 2011, the amount of time the Internet was viewed using mobile devices surpassed all other devices. It was also, not surprisingly, around the same time the sales of tablet-style devices overtook the sale of PCs.

Different websites are visited using different hardware. Some websites are predominately accessed by Internet browsers on desktop computers, while others are accessed using smart phones (e.g. Blackberry, iPhone, etc.). Online community websites like Facebook and Twitter tend to be visited using smart phones, while business-to-business website (e.g. ibm.com) might be viewed more by traditional browsers. The wholesale migration of Web use to mobile devices is clear.

By now, you might have had a chance to look at some Google Analytics reports for your own website. One of the reports it offers shows you how many of your visitors used a mobile device – and which types they used – to look at your website, is shown in the sample report in Illustration 34. To get to that report, click Visitors and Mobile Devices, as shown in Illustration 33 on page 183.

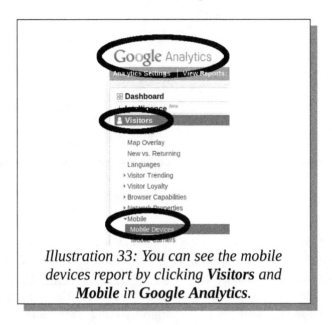

*Illustration 33: You can see the mobile devices report by clicking **Visitors** and **Mobile** in **Google Analytics**.*

Knowing how many of your website visitors are confined to a view the size of a smart phone will help you decide if you need smaller pages on your website to cater for such visitors. At the very least, it is worth browsing your own website with a smart phone to get a sense of what the visitor experience might be and if there are any obstacles to their making contact with you.

Operating System	None	Visits ↓
1. iPhone		183
2. iPad		58
3. Android		29
4. BlackBerry		12
5. iPod		5

Illustration 34: Google Analytics report (Visitors/Mobile/Mobile Devices)

Some search engines (Google, Bing, etc.) offer a free mobile-friendly page on their local search features. To see an example of this, go to www.driscollplumbing.com and click the "*on a smartphone?*" link just below the menu bar. The page you will see is provided by Bing. It is more suited to website owners whose customers are local. That is, they are generally within driving distance of the business.

90: Flash animations versus GIF animations

Effort: ●●○○○   Cost: $0   Reward: ★★☆☆☆

Not every Web browsing device will display web pages containing Flash animations properly. Apple does not support – as of late 2011 – Flash animations in its tablet iPad, and other browsers may not be configured properly for your website's Flash animations to be experienced properly. Just recently I saw an ad for a competitor to the iPad (which does not support Flash animations) extolling the benefits of their support for Flash. I expect, sometime soon Apple will surrender to the popularity of Flash, just the way Microsoft eventually surrendered to the PDF standard.

If such tablet users (iPad users in particular) represent an important segment of your target market, you might reconsider the use of Flash in favor of GIF animations, if indeed you need animations. GIF images are supported by all browsers and tend to look the same across all platforms and browsers. They are also relatively lightweight and easy to produce.

Another alternative to both Flash and GIF animations is to use Javascript to transition images from one to another, creating a "slide show" within a page, as illustrated on the front page of the website www.MajorAnalysis.com.

To see the percentage of visitors to your website that do not support Flash, Google Analytics offers a report under *Browser Capabilities / Flash Versions*, as shown in Illustration 35 on page 186.

Flash Versions	Site Usage	Goal Set 1	
Java Support			

Network Properties	Visits	Pages/Visit		Avg. Time
Mobile	**3,079**	**3.40**		Site
User Defined				**00:02:3**
Custom Variables	% of Site Total:	Site Avg: 3.40		Site Avg: 00:
Traffic Sources	100.00%	(0.00%)		(0.00%)

	Flash Version	None ⌄	Visits ▾ ↓	Visits
Content				
Goals				
	1. ■ 10.1 r102		658	21.37%
Custom Reporting	2. ■ 10.1 r85		515	16.73%
	3. ■ 10.0 r22		445	14.45%
Customizations	4. (not set)		310	10.07%
Custom Reports	5. ■ 10.2 r152		252	8.18%
Advanced Segments	6. ■ 10.3 r181		168	5.46%
Intelligence beta	7. ■ 10.1 r53		166	5.39%
Email	8. 10.0 r45		76	2.47%
lp Resources	9. 10.1 r82		70	2.27%
About this Report	10. ■ 10.2 r154		68	2.21%
Conversion University				
Common Questions				

Illustration 35: In this example, 10% of the visitors used a browser that did not appear to support Flash.

91: Adding a browser shortcut icon

When you have multiple tabs open in your browser, each tab can have its own icon. That tiny image defaults to something provided by the browser itself, but you can replace it with your own, so that when someone is visiting a page on your website, your icon is displayed instead of the default one.

Why would you have your own icon displayed when someone is viewing a page on your website? Icons are visual cues to reinforce a visitor's orientation; a reminder of what is contained on the page they are looking at. If they bookmark your page, the icon is also remembered, so when they return to their bookmarks, the icon serves as a quick reminder of what your page contains. Such icons also act subconsciously, helping a visitor to remember. What's more, all professional websites display their own icon in place of the default and consequently, it gives that professional finish that your website should take advantage of too.

How to create and install a 'favicon':

Visit the URL:
http://favicon.htmlkit.com/favicon/

Follow the instructions to upload the image you wish to be used as an icon. It will provide you with a ZIP file containing a file called *favicon.ico*. Unzip it and move it to the same directory as the home directory. (You could instead move it to your images directory if you prefer; using the home directory in this example just makes the explanation simpler).

With the file in place, the only thing left to do is add a line of HTML to your home page (or any page on your website) to tell it to use the new icon.

Immediately after the </header> in your HTML, place the following line:

<link rel="shortcut icon" type="image/x-icon" href="http://www.bike-repair-seattle.com/favicon.ico" />

To help avoid typos, you can get a sample of this, already typed in and working on our sample page. Click the View/Source menu and look for the text *favicon.ico*: www.bike-repair-seattle.com

Selling from your website

As a rule-of-thumb, a business that wishes for success on the Web needs either *traffic* or a *hot product* or both. If you have a bed-and-breakfast business that offers the best possible view of Niagara Falls, you have a *hot product*. If you are selling the last two hundred units of Nintendo Thing-a-magig a week before Christmas Day, you have a *hot product*. If you have a million visitors a day passing through your website, you have *traffic*. Companies that have serious traffic coming through their website can make a profit by selling other products for a commission. Companies that have a hot product can find a well-trafficked website and offer a commission to sell their product.

For this section of the book, let's assume you have succeeded in driving traffic to your website. If so, there are a number of ways to profit from this valuable traffic by selling something to those visitors. To prepare for that, your website will need to do one or more of the following:

1. Sell a single product at a time.

2. Use a shopping cart on a shopping cart vendor's website.

3. Sell quantities of different products in a single transaction with an on-site shopping cart.

4. Use a shopping cart on your own website.

5. Sell other people's products, sending visitors to other websites, collecting commissions for sales closed.

In each case, you are using the flow of traffic through your website to generate revenue. We'll look at each case in this chapter, starting on page 191 and you will learn how to make it work on your website.

Today, few companies store their customers' credit card information. Instead, they use a third party to perform the final step in the sale. There are several advantages to you, the small business owner, for doing it this way:

1. You don't have to ask your customers to trust you with such confidential information.

2. You don't have to build the sophisticated online infrastructure required now by federal law for companies who gather such credit card details.

3. You don't need a credit card merchant account.

4. Third Party providers (PayPal, Google, etc.) generally support all major credit cards.

When Google (through Google Checkout) or PayPal process your customers' transactions, the effort required for you to sell product directly on your website is much less than being your own credit card merchant. Depending on how complex your requirements are, you may be up and running – selling product directly from your website – within a few minutes.

1: Selling a single product at a time

If you can adjust the HTML on a page of your website – even if you don't understand it completely – you will be able to add a Buy Now button to your website, which is how you sell individual products. The HTML you add is trivial, and it is provided for you by organizations like Google and PayPal free of charge.

Illustration 36 on page 193 shows where in your PayPal account your Buy Now button can be designed.

Illustration 37 on page 194 shows an example of how options can be added to the Buy Now button.

Once you have designed your Buy Now button, press the "Create Button" button at the bottom of the page. Copy the

Selling from your website

HTML it gives you into a page on your website, and *voilà*, you can now sell that product directly from your website. The money goes into your bank account when the transaction is complete. Note: Google Checkout does require a grace period of a number of days before they transfer the cash to your bank account, but that grace period is eliminated once your account is in good standing for a few months. PayPal puts the cash into your PayPal account, and from there, some restrictions apply relating to the amount and frequency of how the cash can be moved to a regular bank account. Their policies change over time, but their most current requirements are explained in detail as you set up your accounts with them.

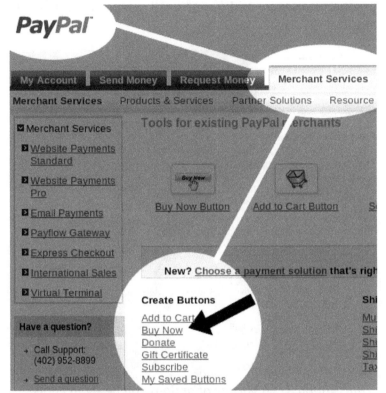

Illustration 36: PayPal feature to create a "Buy Now" button under the Merchant Services menu.

How does it work? When you were logged in to PayPal, it had all of your merchant information to build your Buy Now button. Once you pressed Create Button, the code it generated for you contained everything needed to tie your visitor's transaction back to your own PayPal merchant account. This method of accepting payments for service or products is used by millions of small companies around the world.

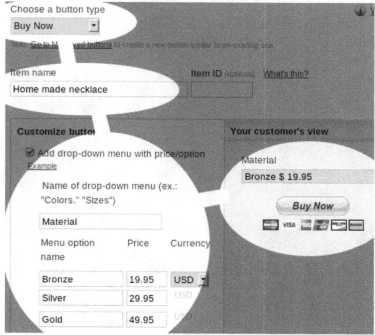

Illustration 37: A variety of options can be set to change the appearance and functioning of the Buy Now button. This image shows how different prices can be set for specific product variations.

2: Using a shopping cart on a shopping cart vendor's website

Effort: ●●○○○○	Cost: $0	Reward: ★★

What does this mean? Rather than house the shopping cart within your own website – which used to be complicated in the past, but is much easier to do today – you can use the shopping cart features of a company that builds all the functionality for you. The problem is, asking your visitors to purchase your products by clicking through to another website may send a brand message that conflicts with your intentions. It can send the message *we are so small we can't afford to handle our own sales* and/or dilute your branding efforts by introducing the brand of the company handling the sale for you. On the other hand, if your business really is very small, it might actually help close the sale by showing your customer their transaction is securely handled by such-and-such corporation. Certainly, in the case of Google and PayPal handling the credit card part of your sale, you are likely to benefit from the implied security offered by either of those two powerful brands, but in this action item, we are talking only about the entire shopping experience being handled by a third party.

How does it work?

Go to Google and search for *ecommerce services*. There are countless companies out there who provide such a service. Each has its own way of doing it, but in a nutshell, the shopping cart is on *their* website, not yours. It makes it easier for you, but the sales transaction is out of your hands and the service usually costs money.

3: Selling multiple units and products

Effort: ●●●○○ | Cost: $0 | Reward: ★★★☆☆

This is slightly more involved than simply adding a Buy Now button, but is still not that complicated. The HTML code is usually generated for you, so you only need to work out where it is to be inserted into your website.

There are dozens, if not hundreds, of website shopping carts available on the Web, many of which are free, and many of them are easy to add to your website.

It is typical of new technologies that hundreds, if not thousands, of potential solutions emerge onto the market in the early stages, and some time later, the list of solutions is whittled down to a small number of survivors. For this reason, I expect most of the current website shopping cart solutions on the market to be gone soon, so selecting one that is likely to be around ten years from now is probably a good idea.

I will talk about two of the more common of them that are easy to use and are free: Google Checkout and PayPal.

Selling more than one product at a time means you need an actual shopping cart (versus a buy-one-at-a-time feature), so I will cover that here too.

Google Checkout Shopping Cart

Google Checkout is an attractive product for many reasons. One drawback – for the moment at least – is that people are not as familiar with it as they are with PayPal's Shopping Cart. Still, it is worth noting that it is supported by an impressive and growing after-sale feature set that few other solutions can match:

1. Seamless integration into Google Analytics means you can view your visitors' shopping cart behavior using the same tool you use to examine their general behavior elsewhere in your website.

2. From Shopping Cart to bank account: You can be up and running with your first shopping cart, complete with integration of revenue going directly into a bank account that you specify, within a matter of minutes.

3. No credit card merchant account requirement: Google is the actual merchant for customers' purchases on your website. There are the usual credit card fees, but you will have those no matter what credit card processing solution you choose. Google supports all major credit cards, and people are generally more comfortable with giving Google their credit card information than they are giving it to a relatively obscure merchant.

4. Google Shopping Cart is highly customizable. You can change the shape, size, color and behavior of it, if you need to.

An example of the Google checkout Shopping cart in action may be seen at www.lmatters.com

PayPal Shopping Cart

PayPal also offers a shopping cart. Although it could be said it is not as sophisticated as the Google Checkout Shopping Cart, it is a little easier to implement. And the big advantage it has is that it is well established on the Internet already. Most people who have made purchases on the Web have already done so using a PayPal Shopping Cart solution. This broad familiarity may increase the likelihood that a visitor will buy product directly from your website, especially if they already have a PayPal account.

To create the code for an **Add to Cart Button** on your own website, you must first log into your PayPal account, click the Merchant Services section. Under it, you have the choice to click Add to Cart Button, as shown in Illustration 38, below. From there, you can specify product price, description, options, and so on, before pressing the "Create Button" button. (My apologies for the overuse of the word *button*!)

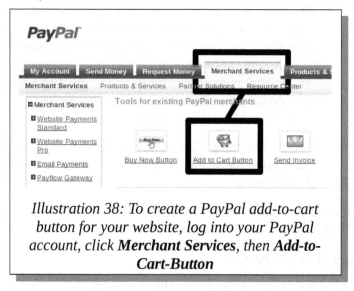

*Illustration 38: To create a PayPal add-to-cart button for your website, log into your PayPal account, click **Merchant Services**, then **Add-to-Cart-Button***

Unlike the Google Checkout Shopping Cart solution, the PayPal Shopping Cart solution does not store its shopping cart on your website. As your website visitor adds each item to the shopping cart, they are taken to a page on the PayPal website where they see all the items they have added to their shopping cart so far. The good thing about this is, your visitors get a clear understanding that their information is secure, as the PayPal secure payments logo is clearly displayed (see bottom of Illustration 39 on page 200), as is the https ('s' meaning secure) in the address bar. This solution is ideal for very small businesses, such as one-person, work-from-home organizations. There is also no cost associated with setting all of this up.

The downside with PayPal Shopping Cart – or perhaps PayPal in general – is that it sends a "we are small" message to potential customers. On the other hand, this may be the precise message you wish to portray. Whatever your branding aspirations are, there is no doubt about the simplicity and ease-of-installation with this solution. You can be up and running with PayPal Shopping Cart in a matter of minutes.

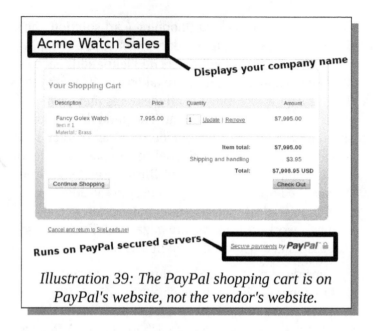

Illustration 39: The PayPal shopping cart is on PayPal's website, not the vendor's website.

4: Using an all-in website hosting & solution provider

Google Checkout Shopping Cart and PayPal Shopping Cart are just two of the hundreds of available solutions you can use to handle sales on your own website. There are third party shopping cart solutions to handle just about any type of complex requirement you might have. There are also entire website solutions that come with built-in shopping cart support. For example, homestead.com offers a click-by-click, build your own website solution that can – if you're not too worried about complex requirements – have an entire website up and running, complete with product inventory management and shopping cart, in an afternoon.

Another provider, alice.com, offers a variation on the external shopping cart model by allowing visitors to place an order from multiple vendors (one of which could be your business) in a single shopping basket. This has the advantage of your product being – potentially – introduced to new customers who are far along in the buying process.

The challenge with moving more and more of your website presence to a solution controlled by such third party vendors is that you lose control. *Control of what,* you might ask. Control of many of the factors that cause search engines to find you and display your website at the top of organic search results, which is possibly the single most important purpose of a website for a small company. Still, it might fit perfectly with your business model, as clearly, many companies have already had huge success with it.

When you examine any such solution, ask yourself, *how much does this solution help me increase targeted traffic to my website or increase lead generation?* Or, *does it grow my business in a way that supports my business plan?*

The challenge – and the opportunity – of website traffic and lead generation is that each organization has different requirements, making it all but impossible to adopt a one-size-fits-all approach. That is, when you hope to generate traffic and leads on your own website. When I look at the kind of solutions offered by companies catering to tens of thousands of tiny companies, each at a low cost, it is hard to believe their promises of getting each customer to the top of search results to any meaningful degree. For local search challenges, yes, it is definitely easier to enumerate the steps necessary to get a website to appear at the top of search results, but for a company with national or global aspirations, a lot of work is required. Even if you are a one-person company selling your wares to the whole world from your kitchen table, you may have *thousands* of competitors, each vying to appear at the top of organic search results. For that reason, you need minute control over each and every field within the pages of your website. Page titles, meta keywords, headers, page names, alt texts and dozens of other elements – spelled out in the first half of this book – contribute to your chances of your web pages being matched up with search words that people are actually using. If the program that builds your website does not allow control over all or most of those elements, you are less likely to appear at the top. In addition, if such website provider companies offer the same promise – for example, to dozens of home-made jewelry companies – how can they *all* appear at the top of search results?!

The journey towards appearing at the top of search results is almost always best served with a *long keyword strategy* (as explained on 28) – which implies every business's needs are examined and executed on a case-by-case basis – and it is unlikely that a large company can offer a one-size-fits-all solution that really works. If you want your website to work for you, you need control over all of its contents and structure, so that it stands out from the crowd. It's just like the way a successful business owner builds a great business: they leave nothing important to chance.

Wrapping up

My wish with this book was to give you, the reader, every last piece of knowledge I have – at least at the time of typing this – about how to get more visitors to your website and how to convert more of them to high quality sales leads. I know – because I've been there – that most small companies don't have lots of cash to throw at their website. Maybe you do have extra cash, but you would prefer to do as much as possible without spending money first, right? For that reason, I listed the zero-cost items first.

Wrapping up

With some effort and a little luck, you may be seeing the first fruits of your labors by now. For some businesses, the phone starts to ring within a few days of making a dozen changes. For others, it takes months or more. For pretty much every website I've ever been involved in, it is just a matter of time and effort before you see your website appear on Page One of search results and for the first solid leads to be in your hand some time after that.

Just like the submarine crew I talked about on page 12, at some point your web presence achieves positive buoyancy and the leads begin to arrive. *When* that will happen depends on what kind of shape you are in to begin with, what your competitive landscape looks like and how much work you are prepared to put into it. Rest assured, though, the technology involved is not that complex. It is mostly a question of doing a hundred or so straightforward things right and biding your time.

Still, in this high tech Internet world of ours, new stuff arrives every day it seems. The ink in this book will hardly have the chance to dry before I will learn something new I'd like to share with you. And for that, you will always find me at www.sboseries.com. Please visit me there and join in the conversation if you wish.

Thank you, my good reader, for buying this book and trusting me with some of your hard-earned money. I wish you the best of luck.

Liam Scanlan

Small Business Owner Series
www.sboseries.com

Glossary

Backlink

A *backlink* – or *inbound link* – is something on a web page *outside* of your website which, when clicked, takes the browser to *your* website. For example, if you answered a question on the Bank of America Small Business Forum and below your answer, you linked your name to the address (www.mybigbiz.com) of your own business's website, that link you created on the B of A forum would be considered a *backlink*.

A *backlink* to your website can also be described as an *outbound link* by the owner of the website it is coming from. And when you create a link on your website to point to a page on someone else's, from your perspective, that is an *outbound link*.

Web Content Management System

A Web Content Management System (WCM) is a program that runs on the server - or close to the server – that hosts your website. It takes care of the security, storage, organization, integrity and publication of the website contents. It is also referred to as a CMS (Content Management System), but lately, the term WCM has been used more, probably because CMS is also the acronym for *Contact* Management System. Usually, a WCM offers a way to add, change, delete and schedule for publication, pages and other data on the website.

There are hundreds, perhaps thousands, of WCMs on the market, and new ones are arriving all the time. A small handful of them, however, account for the publication of probably 95% of all websites created using a WCM. That handful are WordPress, Joomla, Drupal. Coming in close behind them are Magento, ExpressionEngine and a few others.

Some WCMs are free, meaning you can use them without paying for them. Others require that you pay a license fee; some per website, others per installation covering many websites. Prices range mostly between two hundred dollars and about four or five hundred. There are also some specialized WCMs on the market that can cost tens of thousands of dollars.

Depending on what you are trying to achieve with your website presence, one of these WCMs may meet your requirements.

It is important to know that since the turn of the century, there has been a significant migration of website development towards the use of WCMs. Before that, people built websites mostly on a desktop computer using a "HTML Editor" (e.g. FrontPage, Home Site, Dreamweaver) and manually uploaded the website and its objects to a web server. That process was error prone and lacked the security and multi-contributor features available today in an industrial strength WCM like the leading products listed above.

The reason there are so many WCMs on the market is, many companies develop their own from scratch only to realize they have the basis of a potentially valuable product, and proceed then to try to market it against the many established players out there. In addition, their investment in their own home-grown WCM, as well as their website's dependence upon it, makes it difficult to support and increasingly hard for the website to compete with websites developed using a market-established and fast-growing WCM.

Every organization committed to the success of its web presence will use an established, market-tested and well-supported Web Content Management System to build and maintain its website.

Google PageRank

Google PageRank is a score that Google gives a web page. It is based on many factors, among which are the quality of the website that contains it, the age of the domain, how many links point to it, how active the website is and many other factors. Outside of a small handful of people inside Google, no one knows for sure how exactly Google PageRank is calculated, but it is safe to assume that factors suggesting a page is valuable are also likely to contribute to its PageRank.

Note that PageRank is not an arithmetic scale, but rather, a *logarithmic* one. A PageRank of 8 might be five to ten times more valuable than a PageRank of 7. Whatever number of pages there are on the Internet – some say it is around ten billion – most of them have a PageRank of zero. Perhaps one tenth as many have a PageRank of 1, one tenth of those a PageRank of 2, and so on, until you get to a very small number with a PageRank of 10.

Being a logarithmic measure, PageRank behaves like the Richter Scale which measures how severe an Earthquake is. A 6.0 earthquake in Seattle would give you just a little scare, while a 9.0 would level the city. An earthquake of magnitude 9 is one thousand times more powerful than one of magnitude 6. A web page with a Google PageRank of 9 might have a *search engine stickiness* a thousand times greater than a page with a PageRank of 6.

Google Toolbar

Google Toolbar is a free plug-in that works in most browsers. A quick Web search for it will lead you to Google's page where you can install it into your browser with just a few clicks. Toolbar gives you a number of neat features, available as a set of buttons in your browser window.

Illustration 40 shows how to display PageRank on the Toolbar. Click the options button (a wrench icon on the right of the Toolbar) and check PageRank. Close the Options window and visit a page you would like to see PageRank for. Illustration 41 Shows the PageRank for the web page the browser is currently on.

Illustration 40: After Google Toolbar has been installed, you can add Google PageRank to it under Toobar options.

Illustration 41: Google Toolbar indicating the PageRank of the web page you are visiting.

HTML (Hyper Text Markup Language)

This is the English-looking language that is used to construct pages on a website. HTML is used to control the sections of a web page and some of its appearance. It specifies how, for example, images should appear when viewed in a browser. Here is an example of some HMTL:

```
<title>Welcome to Acme Products</title>
<img src="www.ibm.com/logo.jpg">
<meta name="keywords" content="cycle, sales,
repair" />
```

For web pages, HTML is the overlord of how everything else behaves. Embedded in the HTML you can find scripting languages and other fascinating technical stuff going on.

img tag

The *img* tag is used in HTML to tell the browser to display an image. For example:

```
<img src="mywebsite.com/images/bicycle.jpg">
```

Within the opening '<' and the closing '>' lies everything the browser needs to know about displaying the image.

Here is a more typical example of the use of the *img* tag, complete with instructions on what to display if the image can't be loaded and what to display when a mouse is moved over the image. We use the words *src, alt* and *title* to do it:

```
<img src="mywebsite.com/images/bicycle.jpg"
alt="display this if image doesn't load" title="display
this if a mouse moves over the image">
```

Nameservers

Nameservers are hosted by your website hosting company and contain a lookup table of websites that are hosted on their associated website server. A nameserver is like a list at a hotel reception that holds the name and room number of each guest staying at the hotel. When you buy a domain name (e.g. myfancystore.com) you point it to at least one nameserver which in turn, tells where on the server the website is located.

Nameservers are often used in pairs. If the first one gives no response, the website can also be found at the second location.

An example of a nameserver pair might be:

ns621.websitewelcome.com
ns622.websitewelcome.com

Organic search results

Any part of search results that is not an advertisement or promotion. Usually, it is the unshaded area of search results. It is highly advantageous for your web pages to appear there – and as high as possible – because it is perceived as an objective positive assessment by search engines. In other words, search engines display pages there when they believe those pages are the best matches for the search words entered by the person looking for solutions like yours.

Permanent 301 Redirect

Added to a website server, it specifies that a specific web address (URL) now lives at a new location.

For example, when the company EMC acquired the company Legato, they came into possession of Legato's domain name (legato.com). EMC added a Permanent 301 Redirect for legato.com to thereafter "point" to a new location – a page somewhere on EMC's own website. Use your browser to visit www.legato.com to see it in effect.

A *Permanent 301 Redirect* tells browsers and other online servers to update their bookmarks to the new location. It takes a couple of minutes to add a *Permanent 301 Redirect*, and it is done by your website administrator through the website's Control Panel. Illustration 42 Shows an example of an entire domain name being redirected to a website with a different domain name.

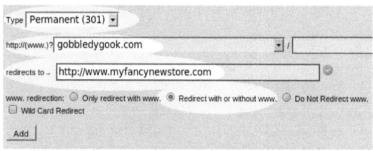

Illustration 42: A screenshot of a Permanent 301 Redirect being added through a website's Control Panel

Registrar

Loosely speaking, the U.S. government allows a selection of companies to issue licenses for the yearly ownership of domain names. Those select companies are called *Registrars*. Examples of Registrars are: GoDaddy.com, Tucows.com, NetworkSolutions.com. To buy a domain name for a year or more, you must go through a Registrar. Even IBM or Apple can't issue their own domain licenses. IBM uses NetworkSolutions.com for its ibm.com domain; Apple Computer uses MarkMonitor.com for its apple.com domain name.

You can see who the current Registrar is for a domain name by going to www.internic.net, clicking the Whois tab at the top of the screen, typing the domain name (e.g. sboseries.com) and pressing enter. In about ten seconds, a report will display showing Registrar. For example *Registrar: Network Solutions*.

Search Engine Optimization

Search Engine Optimization (SEO) is the activities you engage in to make pages on your website appear higher up in *organic search results* when people search for a solution like yours. The desired effect of SEO is to increase the number of visitors that come to your website. SEO satisfies the first of three distinct stages of generating revenue on the Web. The three stages are: **Attract**, **Engage**, **Close**.

Search engine stickiness

Search engine stickiness is a term I use to describe how attracted search engines are to a web page or website. The more "sticky" a page is, the earlier it will appear in search results. The home page of the New York Times, for example, is stickier than a web page containing a lowly posting on a neglected blog.

One quick way of determining how sticky a website might be is to examine it using www.WebsiteGrader.com, which will give you a percentile score of how the entire website fares compared to millions of other websites. The higher the score there, the more *sticky* the website is likely to be, and thus, links from it are more likely to be of value to you. If you need to know the search engine stickiness of a specific page, install the Google Toolbar into your browser and check the box to display Google PageRank. View the page you are interested in and see what PageRank is displayed on the Google Toolbar. It is only a rough guide, but Google PageRank – which is explained on page 207 – is another measure of how sticky a web page is.

Semantically related keywords

Semantically related keywords, in the context of how search works, are words that are found most often together. For example, when the word *couch* is found on a web page, the word *table* is more likely to be found than it would be if *couch* were not on the page; when the words *Arizona, California, Nevada, Oregon* and *Washington* are found on a page, the likelihood of the word *Montana* being on the that page is higher.

This is significant because search engines can match your web page with a set of search words even though those exact search words do not appear on your web page. For example, if someone searches using the three words *sofa, stool, chair*, a search engine might return a web page containing the words *couch, armchair* and *bench*. That is because search engines – Google in particular – match words often found in the same context as the ones you are searching for. They do this because it often provides a better set of search results, one that respects the *meaning* of why a person searches, rather than executing an exact word match every time.

Squeeze Page

A *Squeeze Page* is a web page optimized for the extraction of contact details from a visitor to that web page.

For example, you might place an online ad that offers a free instructional golf video for everyone who enters their contact details into the *Squeeze Page*.

Target Landing Pages are sometimes also *Squeeze Pages*, although it is more common that a *Squeeze Page* is not optimized for organic search results, but is dedicated to the sole purpose of extracting contact information. Thus, it is more likely to be the page someone lands on when they click an ad or when they click a link in an email they received as a part of an email marketing campaign.

Considering the fact that the primary purpose of the website of the vast majority of small business websites is to generate leads, the *Squeeze Page* plays a significant role.

A *Squeeze Page* usually has *no exit hyperlinks*. That is, once the visitor has arrived at the page, they can either surrender their contact information or leave the website.

There is a lot of psychology behind the construction of a Squeeze Page. Colors, form, success stories, videos and images all contribute to the "sell", and professional marketers focus everything on the page towards getting that contact information – or selling a product immediately – before the visitor loses interest and wanders off.

URL (Uniform Resource Locater)

A URL, sometimes pronounced "Earl", but usually as "U-R-L" is a web object's address on the Internet. The home page to your organization's website has a straightforward URL. It might look something like http://www.myfancybusiness.com. Other URLs are more complicated. The URL pointing to a posting on someone's account in Facebook might be long.

URLs are used to bookmark favorite pages, link from one web page to another, follow the steps of an online order or any number of other purposes.

Here are a few examples of different types of URL:

http://www.ibm.com

http://www.siteleads.net/bm/blog

https://siteleads.net/clientview?5049

As you can see, many different needs can be satisfied from within the URL, for example, specifying a client ID to take the visitor to a specific account page of a website (as in the last of the four examples, above).

Alphabetical Index

Glossary

Glossary